PEOPLE AROUND THE WORLD

Antony Mason

KINGFISHER

Contents

Net gains

*Fishermen in Lake Inle in Myanmar
(Burma) drop cylindrically shaped
nets to the bottom of the lake, then
spear the fish caught in the nets.*

PEOPLE
AROUND
THE WORLD

Edited and designed by Toucan Books Limited, London
Editorial consultant Keith Lye

For Kingfisher Publications Plc
Managing editor Melissa Fairley
Editorial Sheila Clewley
Art director Mike Davis
DTP co-ordinator Sarah Pfitzner
Production controller Debbie Otter
Picture research Rachael Swann

KINGFISHER

Kingfisher Publications Plc
New Penderel House,
283-288 High Holborn,
London WC1V 7HZ

www.kingfisherpub.com

First published by Kingfisher Publications Plc 2002

1TR/TWP/CLSN(CLSN)i/130MA

10 9 8 7 6 5 4 3 2 1

A CIP catalogue record for this book is available from the
British Library.

ISBN 0 7534 0718 3

Colour separations by Colourscan
Printed in Singapore

Collecting water

*For many people, getting clean water involves more
than turning on a tap. These school children in Zimbabwe
in Africa are queuing at the village water pump.*

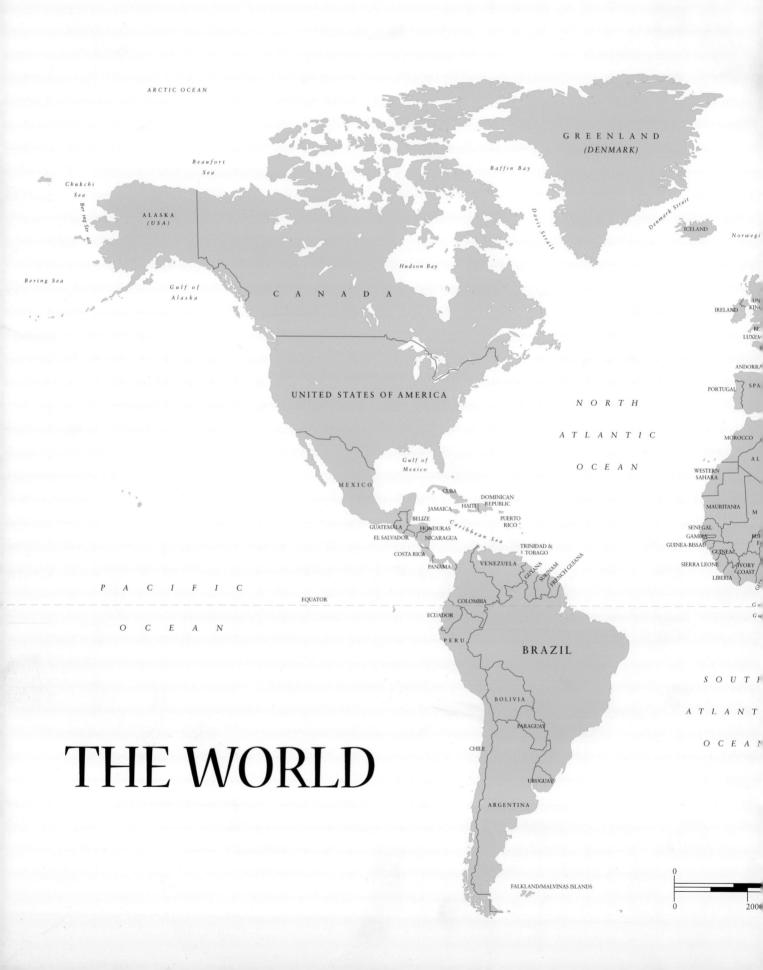

ARCTIC OCEAN

Beaufort Sea

Chukchi Sea

Baffin Bay

GREENLAND
(DENMARK)

Davis Strait

Denmark Strait

ICELAND

Norwegi

ALASKA
(USA)

Bering Str ait

Bering Sea

Gulf of Alaska

Hudson Bay

C A N A D A

IRELAND

UN
KING

BE
LUXEM

ANDORRA

PORTUGAL   SPA

UNITED STATES OF AMERICA

N O R T H

A T L A N T I C

O C E A N

MOROCCO

WESTERN
SAHARA

AL

Gulf of Mexico

M E X I C O

CUBA

DOMINICAN
REPUBLIC

JAMAICA   HAITI

PUERTO
RICO

MAURITANIA

BELIZE

GUATEMALA

HONDURAS

EL SALVADOR   NICARAGUA

Caribbean Sea

SENEGAL

GAMBIA

GUINEA-BISSAU

GUINEA

BEI

FA

COSTA RICA

TRINIDAD &
TOBAGO

SIERRA LEONE

LIBERIA

IVORY
COAST

PANAMA

VENEZUELA

GUYANA

SURINAM

FRENCH GUIANA

P A C I F I C

EQUATOR

COLOMBIA

G

G

ECUADOR

O C E A N

P E R U

BRAZIL

S O U T H

A T L A N T

O C E A N

BOLIVIA

PARAGUAY

THE WORLD

CHILE

URUGUAY

ARGENTINA

FALKLAND/MALVINAS ISLANDS

0

0   2000

ARCTIC OCEAN

ARCTIC OCEAN

Laptev Sea

East
Siberian
Sea

Barents Sea

Kara Sea

Chukchi
Sea

WAY

SWEDEN   FINLAND

R   U   S   S   I   A

Bering Strait

ESTONIA
LATVIA
LITHUANIA
RUSSIA

Baltic Sea

BELARUS

Sea of
Okhotsk

Bering Sea

ARK

HERLANDS

ANY

POLAND

CZECH
REP.
SLOVAK
REP.

UKRAINE

KAZAKHSTAN

MONGOLIA

Sea of
Japan

I.

HUNGARY

MOLDOVA

ROMANIA

CROATIA

OVIN

UNION OF
SERBIA AND
MONTENEGRO
MACEDONIA

BULGARIA

Black Sea

GEORGIA

Caspian Sea

Aral
Sea

KYRGYZSTAN

C   H   I   N   A

NORTH
KOREA

SOUTH
KOREA

JAPAN

EGOVIN

ITALY

ALBANIA

GREECE

ARMENIA

UZBEKISTAN

TURKMENISTAN

TURKEY

AZERBAIJAN

TAJIKISTAN

Yellow
Sea

iterranean Sea

CYPRUS
LEBANON
ISRAEL

SYRIA

IRAQ

I   R   A   N

AFGHANISTAN

East
China Sea

NISIA

JORDAN

KUWAIT

PAKISTAN

NEPAL

BHUTAN

TAIWAN

P   A   C   I   F   I   C

LIBYA

EGYPT

Red Sea

SAUDI
ARABIA

BAHRAIN
QATAR

UNITED
ARAB
EMIRATES

BANGLADESH

I   N   D   I   A

MYNAMAR LAOS

O   C   E   A   N

R

CHAD

OMAN

YEMEN

Bay of
Bengal

THAILAND

VIETNAM

South
China
Sea

ERITREA

SUDAN

Gulf of Aden

A

DJIBOUTI

CAMBODIA

PHILIPPINES

Philippine Sea

CENTRAL
AFRICAN
REPUBLIC

ETHIOPIA

SOMALIA

SRI
LANKA

ROON

EQUATORIAL
GUINEA

ON

CONGO

UGANDA

KENYA

BRUNEI

MALAYSIA

Celebes
Sea

DEMOCRATIC
REPUBLIC OF
CONGO

RWANDA
BURUNDI

TANZANIA

I   N   D   I   A   N

I   N   D   O   N   E   S   I   A

PAPUA
NEW
GUINEA

SOLOMON
ISLANDS

O   C   E   A   N

ANGOLA

ZAMBIA

MALAWI

Coral Sea

VANUATU

FIJI

MOZAMBIQUE

MADAGASCAR

Mozambique Channel

MAURITIUS

NEW CALEDONIA

NAMIBIA

ZIMBABWE

RÉUNION

BOTSWANA

SWAZILAND

A   U   S   T   R   A   L   I   A

LESOTHO

SOUTH
AFRICA

N

Tasman Sea

NEW
ZEALAND

4000   6000   8000 Miles (at equator)

4000   6000   8000   10 000   12 000 Kilometres (at equator)

INTRODUCTION

When astronauts look down upon earth from space they often remark on how beautiful it appears – a spinning jewel of blue and green and wispy cloud surrounded by endless, velvety darkness.

More remarkable though is the dazzling variety of people within each continent. In small clearings in the Amazon rainforest of Brazil, there are people who follow a way of life that has barely changed for thousands of years, while the Brazilian city streets of São Paulo throb with traffic and shoppers in pursuit of the latest fashions.

In Bangalore in India, some of the world's leading computer experts tap away at their keyboards in air-conditioned offices, while in monasteries in valleys high in the Himalayas, Buddhist monks use ancient knowledge and chants in their search for eternal peace.

In Canada, farmers harvest immense fields of ripe wheat with fleets of combine harvesters, while lone Inuit hunters set out across the ice with their rifles and harpoons to catch seals.

From space, astronauts can see all the geographical features of each continent – the coastlines, the plains, the mountains and valleys, the deserts and the icecaps surrounding the Poles. Geography explains much about why people in certain parts of the world lead such different lives. Landscape and climate determine what grows in each region, what people can eat and how they can survive.

Cultural beginnings

Human beings like us have existed for about 100,000 years. Civilization and the complex world of cities, trade, government, military power, organized religion, writing and art, have existed for about 7,000 years. Over these long periods of time, people have developed their own clear ideas about how best to live in their lands – not just what to grow and eat, but also what clothes to wear, what kind of houses to build, what language to speak, what gods to worship, what musical instruments to play and what games to enjoy. In other words, they have evolved their own cultures.

Isolated communities, with little or no contact with the rest of the world, develop very distinctive patterns of life. For example, in Papua New Guinea, there are numerous remote villages in the mountains – so remote that many have developed their own language, which even people living in the next valley cannot understand. As a result, Papua New Guinea has more than 700 languages.

Global influence

Most communities have had contact with the outside world for thousands of years, through trade, travel, conquest and

Mountain land

The small country of Nepal lies in the Himalaya Mountains and is home to the world's highest peak – Mount Everest.

migration. This contact with other peoples has a very strong influence on how we lead our own lives.

Potatoes, tomatoes and chocolate, for instance, were unknown to the world outside the Americas before the arrival of European explorers in the 16th century. Now, through the process of trade, they are found all around the world. Ideas and religions also travel around the world. Indian traders arriving by sea brought Islam to South-east Asia in the 13th century.

The global influence of cultures has speeded up in recent years, through developments in transport and communications. Now mangoes and other tropical fruit can be flown across the world – one day they are on a tree in Pakistan, and a couple of days later they are on the shelves of supermarkets in Europe. Through satellite communications, we can talk to – even see – someone on the other side of the world.

The effect of sharing ideas and products through trade and communications is that cultures around the world are becoming increasingly similar. Some people are concerned by this, and feel that many unique cultures are under threat. But in many cases, this process, known as 'globalization', looks like progress. The lives of many millions of people have been made considerably better through modern medicine, which was largely developed in the Western world. But the impact of exploration and industrial development in remote regions has also exposed native populations to new diseases against which they have no natural resistence, and the adoption of new ways of life can be at the expense of local traditions.

Festive fun
At the annual Ati Atihan festival in the Philippines, children dress up in colourful costumes to enjoy the noisy street parties.

International culture

Today, in many parts of the world, everyday culture has an international influence. Modern pop music is a blend of cultures from around the world with roots in Europe, the USA, the Caribbean, South America, Africa, the Middle East and India. Our supermarkets and restaurants are full of food from an even greater range of countries. We may want this variety of food, but it means that our local diets will change and possibly vanish forever.

There are other social and political implications of this

process of globalization. For instance, in most countries of the world, child labour is against the law, and there are welfare systems to protect the poor. But some of the goods, fruit and vegetables imported from other countries may have been made or picked by workers – sometimes children – who earn very low wages. However, some people argue that low pay is better than no pay – many workers would not survive without these meagre wages.

Meanwhile, the population of the world is growing fast. Currently, it stands at more than

School dinners
Japanese school children use chopsticks to eat their meals.

six billion, and is likely to rise by half as much again, to nine billion, by 2050. China's population is 1.2 billion – the same as the population of the entire world just a hundred years ago. This rapid rise in population – largely due to improvements in medicine and better standards of health – is putting increasing pressure on the land and on resources.

Sense of identity

When people and nations feel themselves under pressure and threat – be it from lack of food or water, or from aggression by other nations – they tend to reinforce their sense of identity. They like to define what it is that

Cultural mix

This youth group has been sponsored by the New York Police Department (NYPD). Many similar inner-city schemes are being developed in the USA.

makes them feel different from other peoples or nations. It could be their language, their religion, their land or even the type of food they eat. This identity gives them a sense of place in their world, reflecting their history and origins.

When disputes arise with other nations or groups, people rally around their identity – represented by flags, symbols and national anthems – and this nationalizm can often be the cause of war. Like globalization, a strong sense of cultural and national identity has both advantages and disadvantages.

Struggles and war are an unfortunate by-product of cultural and religious differences – the same differences that supply the immense richness and variety of human life on earth. And all too often conflict can obscure extraordinary achievements found in all parts of the globe.

ARCTIC AND SUBARCTIC

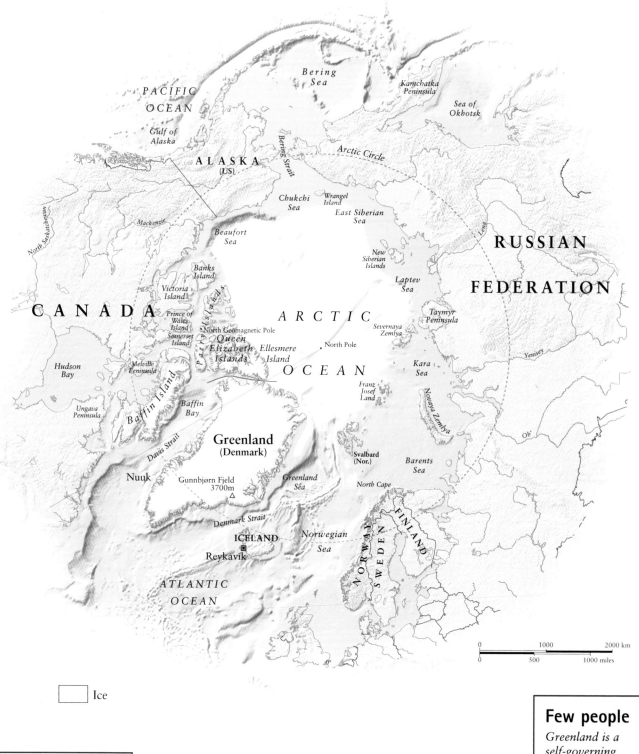

PACIFIC
OCEAN

*Bering
Sea*

*Kamchatka
Peninsula*

*Sea of
Okhotsk*

*Gulf of
Alaska*

ALASKA
(US)

Arctic Circle

Bering Strait

*Chukchi
Sea*

*Wrangel
Island*

*East Siberian
Sea*

Mackenzie

RUSSIAN

North Saskatchewan

*Beaufort
Sea*

*New
Siberian
Islands*

Lena

FEDERATION

*Banks
Island*

*Laptev
Sea*

CANADA

*Victoria
Island*

*Prince of
Wales
Island*

*Somerset
Island*

ARCTIC

North Geomagnetic Pole

*Queen
Elizabeth
Islands*

*Ellesmere
Island*

*Severnaya
Zemlya*

*Taymyr
Peninsula*

• North Pole

OCEAN

Yenisey

*Hudson
Bay*

*Melville
Peninsula*

*Kara
Sea*

*Ungava
Peninsula*

Baffin Island

*Baffin
Bay*

*Franz
Josef
Land*

Novaya Zemlya

Davis Strait

Ob'

Greenland
(Denmark)

*Svalbard
(Nor.)*

*Barents
Sea*

Nuuk

Gunnbjørn Fjeld
3700m △

*Greenland
Sea*

North Cape

Denmark Strait

*Norwegian
Sea*

ICELAND ▫

NORWAY

FINLAND

Reykavík

SWEDEN

*ATLANTIC
OCEAN*

0		1000		2000 km
0	500		1000 miles	

☐ Ice

Northern land

*Canada, Greenland,
Finland, Iceland,
Norway, Russia, Sweden
and Alaska have land
within the Arctic Circle.*

Few people

*Greenland is a
self-governing
province of
Denmark. It is
50 times larger
than Denmark
but only has the
population of
a small town.*

ARCTIC AND SUBARCTIC

The far north of the world is covered by the Arctic Ocean, with sea so cold that much of the surface is coated in ice. As winter approaches, the ice spreads out from the polar icecap and joins up with land, covering the top of the world in a thick white blanket. Despite winter temperatures of −40°C, people have lived in these regions for thousands of years.

Inuit life

The Inuit (previously known as Eskimo) people inhabit Greenland, the northern coasts and islands of Canada, northern Alaska, and the north coast of Russia, where they are known as Yupik.

In the past, the Inuit lived by hunting and fishing. They travelled about in kayaks (canoes) and on sleds drawn by husky dogs, looking for seals, fish and Arctic hares. They dried the meat and fish to preserve it. This gave them food for winter, when they returned to their villages.

The Inuit make warm clothes and boots from animal furs and fish-hooks and harpoons from bones. They have a very strong sense of community, and traditionally rub noses as a greeting.

Keeping warm
Inuit children wear sealskin and caribou jackets to protect them from the harsh Arctic conditions.

Ice fishing

Inuit fishermen make small holes in the ice- and snow-covered lakes and let fishing nets or rods down into the water.

The Inuit are famous for their round ice houses called igloos. These are surprisingly snug inside, but igloos were mostly used as temporary shelters for hunters on the ice, and this is their main use today. In their villages, the Inuit lived in small cabins made of boulders, turf, whalebone and driftwood.

New ways

The lives of the Inuit have changed over the last 50 years. Today, most of them live in houses prefabricated in factories and shipped in by boat, or in modern apartment blocks in the larger towns. They ride snowmobiles instead of husky-sleds, and eat tinned and packet food flown in from towns further south. Some have jobs working in oil fields, or in tourism.

Major efforts are being made to preserve Inuit traditions and their language. Inuktitut is spoken right across the region. In Canada the Inuit have been given their own land called Nunavut ('our land' in Inuktitut) – a vast territory of more than two million km^2 in the north-east.

GREENLAND

Status
Self-governing province
of Denmark
Capital
Nuuk (Godthaab)
Area
2,175,600 km²
Population
13,400
Population density
Less than 0.01 per km²
Life expectancy
64 (m); 72 (f)
Religion
Christianity
Adult literacy rate
100 per cent
Currency
Danish krone

Northern life

*Most people in Greenland live in
towns on the coast, but there are
some smaller settlements where
people live by hunting and fishing.*

EUROPE

ICELAND
Reykjavik ■

ATLANTIC
OCEAN

Faroe Is.

Shetland Is.

Orkney Is.

Outer Hebrides

NORWAY
SWEDEN
FINLAND

Norwegian
Sea

North Cape

Vesterålen

Lofoten

Kola
Peninsula

Oslo ■

Vänern

Stockholm

Helsinki ■

Gulf of Bothnia

Lake
Lad

Gulf of Finland

Tallinn ■

ESTONIA

Saaremaa

Vättern

REP. OF
IRELAND
Dublin ■

UNITED
KINGDOM

North
Sea

DENMARK
COPENHAGEN ■

Öland

LATVIA

RIGA ■

Gotland

Baltic
Sea

Bornholm

LITHUANIA

Russ. Fed.

Vilnius ■

Minsk ■

Celtic
Sea

London ■

NETHERLANDS
Amsterdam ■

Elbe

Berlin ■

GERMANY

Oder

Warsaw ■

POLAND

BELARUS

English Channel

Channel Is.

BELGIUM
Brussels ■

LUXEMBOURG

Kiev ■

UKRAINE

Paris ■

Luxembourg

Prague ■

CZECH
REPUBLIC

Vistula

Loire

Seine

Rhine

Bay of
Biscay

FRANCE

Dnister

SLOVAKIA

Carpathians

Berne ■ Vaduz ■

LIECH.

Vienna ■

Bratislava ■

MOLDO

Garonne

SWITZ.

AUSTRIA

Budapest ■

Massif
Central

Mont Blanc △
4808m

ALPS

SLOVENIA

HUNGARY

Chisinau ■

Ljubljana ■

Pyrenees

Rhône

Po

Zagreb ■

Tisza

ROMANIA

PORTUGAL

Duero

Andorra
La Vella ■ ANDORRA

MONACO

Ligurian
Sea

SAN
MARINO

CROATIA

BOSNIA-
HERZEGOVINA

Belgrade ■

Bucharest ■

Danube

Lisbon ■

Tagus

SPAIN

Madrid ■

Corsica

Appennines

Adriatic Sea

Sarajevo ■

UNION OF
SERBIA AND
MONTENEGRO

BULGARIA

Guadalquivir

Majorca

Ibiza   Minorca

Balearic Islands

Rome ■

VATICAN CITY

Sofia ■

Skopje ■

Tirana ■ MACEDONIA

Strait of Gibraltar

Sardinia

Tyrrhenian
Sea

ITALY

ALBANIA

GREECE

Aegean
Sea

Sicily △ Mt. Etna
3340m

Ionian
Sea

Peloponnese

Athens ■

MALTA
■ Valletta

Rhoo

Crete

Mediterranean
Sea

Novaya Zemlya

Barents Sea

Ural Mountains

Pechora

NorthernDvina

RUSSIAN

FEDERATION

Kama

Volga

Moscow

Ural

Volga

Don

Dnieper

Sea of Azov

CRIMEA

Caspian Sea

Elbrus
△ 5642m

Caucasus

Black Sea

N

	Mountain
	Desert
	Tundra
	Cropland
	Wetland
	Needleleaf forest
	Tropical rainforest
	Temperate grassland
	Ice

0   500   1000 km
0   250   500 miles

Smallest state

The smallest independent state in the world is Vatican City – literally a city inside another city (Rome).

Vast nation

Russia is the world's largest country. A quarter lies in Europe, and the other three-quarters in Asia.

Troubled times

Eastern European states were once controlled by the Soviet Union and now face an uncertain economic future.

The Hexagon

France is the third largest country in Europe. The French call their country L'Hexagone (the hexagon) due to its six-sided shape.

Euro zone

Fifteen countries are currently members of an economic alliance known since 1993 as the European Union. Twelve of these countries share a common currency – the euro.

SCANDINAVIA AND NORTHERN EUROPE

A great hook-shaped piece of land sticks out of Russia, curving around the Baltic Sea. It is divided into three countries – Finland, Sweden and Norway. Across the narrow entrance to the Baltic Sea opposite Sweden lies Denmark, and about 1,000 km into the Atlantic Ocean lies the volcanic island of Iceland. These five countries are known as Scandinavia.

Fjord formation

Norway's famous fjords were formed during the last Ice Age. Glaciers cut through mountains, creating valleys which filled with water.

Fairytale landmark

The Little Mermaid statue in Denmark's capital, Copenhagen, celebrates the work of Denmark's most famous writer, Hans Christian Andersen.

Land of the midnight sun

Each country in north-western Europe has its own language, as well as its own culture and distinctive landscape – but they share a history. Their Viking ancestors were traders and seafarers. Originally from Norway, Sweden and Denmark, the Vikings ventured from their homelands and settled across much of northern Europe from AD 700 to AD 1000. Norway became independent of Sweden only in 1905.

The Scandinavian countries have similar climates. Finland, Sweden, Norway and the very northern tip of Iceland stretch into the Arctic Circle – which means long, dark, snowy winters. For some midsummer days in the Arctic region the sun does not set at all. It is called the 'land of the midnight sun'.

There is good fishing in the North Atlantic and the Baltic, and many people in the cold north make a living from it. It is the main industry in Iceland. There are huge forests in Norway, Sweden and Finland. In fact, almost two-thirds of Finland is covered by forest. The conifer trees are used to make timber, furniture and paper.

The original settlers of the far north, the Lapps (or Sami, as they call themselves), still live by herding reindeer in the Arctic regions of Finland, Sweden and Norway. Further south, in the open countryside of Sweden, farmers grow wheat, oats and potatoes. Denmark is famous for its bacon and dairy products. Norway is more mountainous. Huge mountains rise out of the sea along the west coast, creating fjords (steep-sided sea inlets). On the sheltered coasts of the fjords, warmed by the ocean current called the Gulf Stream, farmers can grow grain, vegetables and fruit, such as apples and pears.

Saunas and smorgasbord

Finland is famous for its saunas – rooms in which water is poured on hot coals so that the heat will make the bather's skin sweat out impurities. The southern part of the country is dotted with lakes, and the Finnish people build special cabins beside the lakes in which to take a sauna. After sitting in the heat for a while, they run out and plunge into the lake's freezing water. In Iceland, hot water is provided direct from the volcanic activity deep beneath the ground. This geothermal energy is tapped to provide heating for houses and greenhouses, and at the Svartseni geothermal power station people can swim outdoors all year round in the man-made Blue Lagoon.

In winter, many people go skiing. There are ski resorts and ski lifts in the mountains of Norway, but cross-country skiing is also popular and especially suitable for the lowlands and lakes of Sweden and Finland. There is also tobogganing and skating.

Sailing, canoeing, fishing and walking are popular summer pastimes. Summer is also the best time to enjoy a traditional Scandinavian meal, or smorgasbord. It is a buffet of dishes such as cold meats, prawns and smoked fish, and slices of marinated salmon, called gravlax.

Lapp tradition

The Lapps (or Sami people) live in northern Norway, Sweden and Finland and some still earn a living by herding reindeer. This Lapp girl is wearing national dress.

Most people live in towns and cities, which lie mainly in the southern part of these countries. None of them is very big. Denmark's capital, Copenhagen, has a population of about 650,000, and Norway's capital, Oslo, has a population of 760,000. The entire population of Iceland numbers just 277,000.

Caring for the people

The countries of north-western Europe are prosperous. They earn money from farming, fishing, forestry and industry. Ships, cars, aeroplanes, mobile phones and furniture are all manufactured in this region. Norway and Denmark have oil, extracted from beneath the North Sea, and Sweden has rich deposits of iron ore, used to make iron and steel.

The countries of north-western Europe are democracies. Iceland has one of the world's oldest parliaments, the Althing, which traces its history back to AD 930, when the island was settled by Norwegian Vikings. Sweden, Norway and Denmark have royal families, and the monarch of each country is head of state. Denmark, Finland and Sweden are members of the European Union, but Norway has voted to remain outside.

Scandinavia has a reputation for the high standard of living of its citizens and for generous government-run healthcare and welfare systems. In the United Nations' Human Development Index – a way of measuring standards of living, based on national income, education and health – the five countries of Scandinavia rank among the top 15 nations in the world.

Warm water

It may have a cool climate, but Iceland is a great place for open-air swimming. Geothermal energy heats the water to temperatures as high as 40°C.

THE BALTIC STATES

Three small countries look out across the Baltic Sea from the coast of northern Europe. Lithuania, Latvia and Estonia are known as the Baltic States, and for much of the 20th century they were part of the Soviet Union. Since 1991, these small, fiercely patriotic countries have begun to enjoy their first taste of independence for over 50 years.

This part of Europe has always been a battle zone for competing nations, with the bigger Baltic countries such as Finland to the north, Poland to the south and Russia to the east. Although Lithuania, Latvia and Estonia broke free from Russia after the Russian Revolution of 1917, the Soviet Union seized them in 1940 and placed them under communist rule, directed from Moscow. Large numbers of people were killed during this period and even more were forcibly moved to other parts of the Soviet Union and replaced by Russians, Ukrainians and Belorussians.

But in 1991, as the Soviet Union crumbled, Lithuania, Latvia and Estonia all declared their independence. This has allowed them to re-open their relationships with surrounding countries, especially Sweden and Finland, on the other side of the Baltic Sea and to trade with the rest of Europe.

Folk tradition

This Latvian girl is wearing traditional folk dress and playing a percussion instrument. Folk music and folk tales are a central part of Latvian culture.

Changing times

Folk tales and legends play a large role in the cultures of the Baltic States – as do music, theatre and dance. The summer festivals in the towns and villages provide showcases for folk singing and dancing. Latvia in particular is famous for its choirs. Rock music, both imported and home-grown, also has an enthusiastic following.

Although religion was discouraged under Soviet rule, Christianity survived. In Estonia and Latvia, most people are Protestants of the Lutheran Church while in Lithuania, the people are fervent Roman Catholics.

Food factories

Food processing is an important industry in the Baltic countries. This woman is preparing fish in an Estonian factory.

The Baltic States are supported by a mixture of farming, forestry and industry. During the Soviet era, huge farms were created and large-scale industries introduced. The farms still produce huge quantities of grain, sugar beet and flax (to make linen), as well as cattle and pigs. The main industries are food processing, electrical engineering and making chemicals and timber products. Tourism is increasingly important to the region. Old cities, such as Riga, Latvia's capital, are now popular holiday destinations.

THE BRITISH ISLES

The British Isles contain two main islands and two independent nations. The larger island is Great Britain. It consists of England, Scotland and Wales. West of Great Britain is Ireland, which is divided into two. The southern part of the island is the independent Republic of Ireland. The north is part of the United Kingdom of Great Britain and Northern Ireland.

A crowded land

Britain is a crowded island. The total population of the United Kingdom is about 59 million, giving a relatively high population density of 246 people per km^2. But there are still large open spaces, particularly in Scotland. The Republic of Ireland, by contrast, has a total population of just 3.7 million, and a population density of 53 people per km^2.

One-third of them live in and around the capital, Dublin.

The British Isles has a mild climate with four distinct seasons. The mildness is due to the Gulf Stream, an ocean current which brings warmth from the Caribbean. Whereas it is possible to grow palm trees in sheltered spots in some parts of the west coasts of Ireland and Scotland, parts of Canada on the same latitude suffer long months of icy winter.

Farming is an important industry in both Britain and Ireland. Ireland is famous for its dairy herds, producing milk, butter and cheese, and is called the 'Emerald Isle' because of its rich green pastures.

Only one per cent of Britons, however, work in agriculture. Nearly 90 per cent of the population live in the towns and cities. Britain was the first industrial nation in the world and its factories produce a huge variety of goods. The number of people working in industry has been declining for many decades because other countries can produce goods far more cheaply than Britain. Today, three-quarters of the workforce, is employed in service industries, such as banking, healthcare and tourism.

Open space

Much of Britain is built up with towns and cities. But there are some beautiful open spaces such as the Lake District, which is in the north-west of England.

Capital destination

Britain's capital, London, is home to the country's parliament. It is also a popular tourist destination, packed with historic sights such as Big Ben.

Cosmopolitan communities

From the 15th century onwards, British explorers travelled to all parts of the world. They created a network of trading links, and gradually took over other countries as colonies in southern Asia, the Far East, the Americas and Africa. By the end of the 19th century, Britain ruled over one-quarter of the world.

Almost all these countries are now independent, but links with Britain remain. When Britain needed more people for its workforce, it encouraged families from the old colonies to emigrate. Today, Britain's cities are home to large immigrant communities, such as Indian, Pakistani, Afro-Caribbean, Chinese and Bangladeshi.

The Republic of Ireland was ruled by Britain until the 1920s. In the past, many Irish people emigrated to other countries to escape poverty. But Ireland's growing economy means it now has to recruit workers from overseas.

Marching past
Pageantry and tradition are an important part of British culture. The Edinburgh Tattoo is an annual Scottish military festival.

Mixed society
British cities are very multicultural. School children learn about the different cultures and religions of their classmates.

THE BRITISH ISLES 29

Church and culture

Britain is a mainly secular (non-religious) society. Although the majority of people are Christian, church attendance is low. Immigrant communities have brought with them their own religions, such as Islam and Hinduism. In contrast to Britain, the Republic of Ireland is strongly Roman Catholic. In Northern Ireland, a bitter dispute between the Protestant majority, loyal to Britain, and the Roman Catholic minority, who want Northern Ireland to be reunited with the Republic of Ireland, has led to violent confrontation lasting over 30 years.

British and Irish culture is a balancing act between preserving a rich heritage and breaking new boundaries. The countryside is dotted with

Industrial town

During the Industrial Revolution in the 19th century, northern cities such as Newcastle grew in size. This area now suffers from high unemployment.

old castles and grand country homes and Britain's royal family and pageantry play a part in state occasions. Local traditions are preserved in each segment of the British Isles. The Scots wear kilts on formal occasions and the Welsh and the Irish have preserved their old languages. The British are also enthusiastic supporters of the sports they invented, including football, rugby and cricket. But the British Isles look to the future. Britain is at the cutting edge of fashion, art and music, and Ireland's booming technology-based economy has earned it the nickname 'Celtic Tiger'.

FRANCE

Stretching from the North Sea and the Atlantic Ocean to the warm Mediterranean Sea in the south, France is the largest country in western Europe. It is a leading industrial power and one of the world's most popular tourist destinations. The country is famous for its culture and cuisine, and its capital, Paris, is home to many fine art galleries and restaurants.

Industry with style

Passengers on France's high-speed TGV trains can gaze out over the landscape to medieval châteaux and ancient cities still crowned with their cathedrals' spires. But France represents a balance between the traditions of the past and the modern world. For example, glass pyramids at the cutting edge of modern architecture have been constructed in the Louvre in Paris. Once a royal palace, the Louvre is now home to paintings and sculptures.

France has a number of major international industries, such as their car manufacturers, Renault, Citroën and Peugeot. But in France, industry and style often go hand in hand. The country's fashion houses and perfumes are famous around the world.

French culture

France is a republic, led by a president and a prime minister. Deputies are elected to represent voters in the

national parliament in Paris. In towns and villages, however, the mayor plays an important role. France is also a member of the European Union, and its currency is the Euro.

One of the great concerns of all levels of French government is to protect and preserve French culture, from its grand traditions of theatre, literature and art, its great cathedrals and galleries, to daily life in the towns and villages. French culture also thrives on the fact that it is very cosmopolitan.

France once had a large empire. It still has territories in the Caribbean and the South Pacific. People from its former colonies have come to live in France. This includes a large population from northern Africa, particularly Algeria. There are also numerous immigrants from other European countries, notably Portugal, Italy and Spain.

Eating out

In the summer, French restaurants and cafés have tables and chairs on the pavement so that families can enjoy dining in the sunshine.

The Louvre

Millions of tourists visit the Louvre in Paris every year. It is home to the world's most famous painting – Leonardo da Vinci's Mona Lisa.

Growing grapes

There are vineyards all over the French countryside. Grapes are cultivated and harvested to make France's famous wines.

Preserving the past

These girls are dressed in regional costume. As part of their school studies, children learn about French history, language and literature.

Fine cuisine

Eating well is an important part of daily life in France. The French pride themselves on the high standard of the food in their markets and their many restaurants. Patés and cold meats, bread and cakes (patisserie), fresh vegetables and fruit are commonly eaten. Other French delicacies include frogs' legs and edible snails. The great interest in eating explains the huge variety of food on sale. There are at least 300 different types of French cheese alone. This far outstrips the number of cheeses produced by any other country.

France has plenty of good, fertile land, and it also has a range of climates, from hot and sunny in the south to cool and wet in the north. This allows the French to grow their own warm-weather crops, such as aubergines, tomatoes, olives and sunflowers, as well as cool-weather vegetables and fruit, such as cabbages and apples. The conditions in much of France are perfect for growing grapes to make their famous wines.

Local loyalties

The French themselves identify strongly with the regions that they come from, which vary from the sun-drenched, hilly landscape of Provence in the south, to the green pastures and orchards of Normandy in the north. Some regions even have their own languages, notably Brittany in the north-west and the island of Corsica in the Mediterranean.

The dynamic mix of food, climate, landscape and history have made France an attractive tourist destination. In fact, France receives more foreign visitors than any other nation – over 70 million every year – more than the population of France itself.

GERMANY

For much of the last century, Germany was divided into democratic West Germany and communist East Germany. In 1990, the two halves were reunited, giving Germany the highest population of any European country – 82 million citizens. Germany is also one of Europe's most successful countries, famous for the very high quality of its industrial products.

Germany's coastlines are bordered by the North and the Baltic Seas. Goods being shipped to and from all parts of the world go through the major trading ports such as Hamburg and Bremerhaven. They are linked to inland European cities by lorries and freight trains. Germany's main industrial centre is the Ruhr Valley in the north-west. The large quantities of coal mined in this region fed the factories in the past, turning iron and steel into heavy machinery and railway engines. These heavy industries have largely disappeared, and today, Germany produces cars, domestic appliances, computers and telecommunications equipment.

Although less than two per cent of Germans work in agriculture, much of Germany remains rural. The rolling landscape is covered by farms and large areas of woodland such as the Black Forest in the south-west. Pig-farming is an important industry, and pork plays a large part in German cooking. A favourite snack is wurst – a large, hot sausage, usually bought from a small roadside stall, and eaten with a roll and a dollop of mustard.

High-rise city

Frankfurt is Germany's financial centre. Much of the city was flattened by bombs during World War II, and since then towering skyscrapers have been built.

The Länder

Germany was once a collection of small states, many of them ruled by princes and bishops, until they were persuaded in 1871 to join together to form one nation. This process, called 'unification', created a centralized government.

Germany is still divided into Länder (states), but now representatives from the various parts of the country meet in the parliament, the Reichstag, in Berlin. The head of the national government is the chancellor and there is also a president, who acts as the head of state.

Each of the Länder has its own proud traditions. For instance, many people still keep a set of traditional costumes to wear at the many local festivals held each year to celebrate the harvest, wine, beer, a local legend or a saint. There are also plenty of regional music festivals. Germany was the birthplace of many of the great composers, including Johann Sebastian Bach, Ludwig van Beethoven and Richard Wagner.

But Germany is a modern nation with a large number of immigrant communities – they make up nine per cent of the population. Many of them, notably from Turkey and the Union of Serbia and Montenegro (formerly Yugoslavia), arrived originally to work in the factories.

Most Germans are Protestant Christians, although Germany is an increasingly secular (non-religious) society. The Länder of Bavaria, in southern Germany, is mainly Roman Catholic, and there are sizeable Muslim and Jewish communities, particularly in the cities.

Reunification

Germany has gone through a huge and sudden change over the past decade, at the end of a traumatic 20th century. In 1900, Germany ruled a large empire, with colonies in various parts of the world, but it lost all of these after its defeat in World War I. Economic turmoil in the 1920s and 1930s made people desperate for change, a situation exploited by Adolf Hitler and his Nazi party, who came to power in 1933. Their grand ambitions to conquer a new empire in Europe led to World War II. After six years of war and the mass destruction of German cities, Germany was defeated.

The country was divided into two parts – East Germany and West Germany.

For 45 years, Germany was ruled as a divided nation, with a heavily patrolled border and fence (part of the so-called 'Iron Curtain') running between the two. West Germany prospered as part of western Europe. East Germany was part of the Soviet empire, and was ruled as a communist state, with few personal freedoms. Although highly productive, its factories were old-fashioned, and its people remained relatively poor.

The collapse of the Soviet empire began in Germany. On an exciting and unforgettable night in November 1989, for the first time in 28 years East Germans were allowed to cross the frontier that divided the city of Berlin. Eight months later, in 1990, Germany was officially reunited as one country. Berlin became the capital again and a massive re-building programme began.

There was a huge gap in living standards between East Germany and West Germany, and, after 45 years of separation, considerable differences in attitudes, which are taking time to resolve. But Germany remains Europe's leading industrial nation. A key member of the European Union, it has abandoned its former currency in favour of the Euro.

The Berlin Wall

In 1961, the communist government of East Germany built a huge wall across Berlin to separate it from the West. In 1989, mass demonstrations led to the government's collapse and the wall was torn down.

Local traditions

Traditional festivals and fairs are held in towns and villages throughout Germany. The streets are decorated with flags and flower displays, and crowds gather to enjoy the dancing and music.

THE LOW COUNTRIES

The set of nations known as the Low Countries – the Netherlands, Belgium and Luxembourg – are called this because, in general, they do not rise high above sea level. In fact, more than a third of the Netherlands is below sea level, because over the centuries farmland has been reclaimed from marshes and the sea by building dykes (sea walls) and canals.

Although each is now independent, the Low Countries are linked together by history. Some 500 years ago they all belonged to Spain. Today, all three countries are democracies with elected parliaments, and all three have ruling royal families – Belgium has a king, the Netherlands a queen, and Luxembourg has a grand duke.

Belgium has three languages. In the northern part, which is called Flanders, the people speak Dutch – similar to the Dutch spoken in the Netherlands. The people in the southern part of the country, called the Walloons, speak French. There are also German-speaking people in the east of the country. The people of Luxembourg speak French, German and their own language, Letzebuergesch. All three nations have sizeable immigrant communities, who live mainly in the cosmopolitan cities.

Trading nations

The Low Countries are prosperous. Luxembourg has the highest Gross Domestic Product (GDP, a way of judging the wealth of a country) per head, per year in the world. All three countries rank among the top 15 nations in the United Nations' Human Development Index (a measurement of quality of life).

They have a long history of trade, going back centuries. This provided the money to build great trading centres, such as the Dutch cities of Amsterdam (the capital of the Netherlands) and Delft, and the Belgian cities of Ghent and Bruges. Today, these represent a curious blend between old and new. Among the old churches and elegant medieval mansions and guild houses, are modern shopping malls and offices. The Dutch prefer their bicycles to their cars – and most cities in the Netherlands have carefully planned cycle paths.

Both the Netherlands and Belgium are major industrial countries, producing cars, domestic appliances, textiles and petrochemicals. Luxembourg is a financial centre for banking, investment and insurance. Brussels, Belgium's main city, is called the 'capital of Europe' because many of the most important offices of the European Union are based there.

The Netherlands has one of the highest population densities in Europe, with about 400 people per km². Many live in the central ring of cities called the Randstad, including Rotterdam, Amsterdam and The Hague. These are in the provinces of North Holland and South Holland, which have given rise to the other name for the Netherlands – Holland.

European centre

The Belgian capital, Brussels, is home to the European Parliament – a directly elected forum for the European Union. Elections are held every five years.

Wind power

Much of the Netherlands is land reclaimed from the sea. Windmills were used to pump water from the land. Today, wind turbines are used to generate electricity.

Tulips and chocolates

Farming plays an important role in the Low Countries. The Netherlands is famous for its dairy farms. Cattle are raised on the rich grass of the polders – the reclaimed land – and their milk is made into cheeses, such as Edam and Gouda. Windmills are used to pump water out of the polders and into the canals, although modern pumps do most of the work these days. The polders of the west coast are used to grow flower bulbs. Millions of tulips, daffodils and other flowers are sold every day of the week at Aalsmeer, the world's largest flower market. Another symbol of the Netherlands is wooden clogs, which some people still wear to protect their feet from the mud and wet.

Belgium is famous for its chocolates, beer, waffles and chips, which are crispy and eaten with mayonnaise. It also has some of the best restaurants in Europe – good food plays a central role in Belgian life.

The Dutch love seafood. One popular local delicacy is herring. It is cured in brine and eaten raw – held by the tail and dropped into the mouth whole.

Flower power

Tulip-growing has been a major business for the Netherlands since the 1600s. Every year about three billion tulip bulbs are produced in the country.

Big cheese

Every week the Dutch town of Alkmaar holds a traditional cheese market. The porters carry cheese on barrows suspended from their shoulders.

THE IBERIAN PENINSULA

The great square-shaped piece of land at the south-western corner of Europe is named after the Iberians, the people who lived here in ancient times, before the Romans conquered the area in the 2nd century BC. Today, the Iberian Peninsula consists of two countries, Spain and Portugal.

Spain occupies the greater part of the peninsula, making it the second largest country in western Europe after France. Its Atlantic coast in the north has a cool climate with plenty of rain, which keeps the countryside green almost all the year. In the north-east the land rises up into a high ridge of rugged mountains, the Pyrenees, which forms a natural frontier with France. In the mountains, sandwiched between the borders of Spain and France, lies the tiny independent state of Andorra – a country of sheep pastures, valley farms and ski-resorts popular with tourists.

Living with the heat

Most of Spain, however, is a hot and dry plateau. To the south and east lies the Mediterranean Sea, with its long sandy beaches and strings of summer holiday resorts. The tourist industry is very important to the Spanish economy, as is agriculture. The hot climate is good for growing tomatoes, fruit, olives, and grapes for wine. During the summer, many people escape the heat of the day by taking a siesta – a long nap after a light lunch – before returning to work in the late afternoon. The main meal of the day is in the evening. It can be grilled meat, or a hearty stew of beans, vegetables, meat and sausage, or perhaps the famous Spanish dish of paella, made of saffron-flavoured rice cooked with prawns, shellfish, chicken and ham. Spanish restaurants often serve tapas (plates of tasty snacks such as cold meats, olives and meat balls).

Fishy dish

Paella is Spain's most famous dish. The rice-based speciality can contain morsels of seafood, meat and vegetables. Every region of Spain has its own distinct method of preparation.

Regional Spain

Spain is divided into regions with contrasting cultures. The Basque country in the north has its own language, which is very different from Spanish. Catalonia, on the north-east coast also has its own language, and it is the main language of Andorra. Asturias on the northern Atlantic coast is green and mountainous. Andalucía in the south is hot and dry, and covered with rocky hills. This last is home to the fiery gypsy flamenco dance, performed to the rhythms of the guitar – an instrument that is associated with Spain.

Trying to hold together this diverse nation has caused problems in the past. In 1936–39, there was a civil war, which resulted in victory for the dictator General Francisco Franco. Shortly after his death in 1975, democracy was restored under King Juan Carlos. Since then, Spain has undergone rapid development, and the cities have become more modern.

Fiestas and bullfights

Fiestas (festivals) are often held to celebrate a local saint – reflecting the fact that most Spaniards are Roman Catholics. Fiestas are colourful events with traditional costumes, funfairs, fireworks and parades.

Many towns and cities have bullrings where bullfighting takes place. They are large, round buildings, with an open arena inside. The matadors (bullfighters) subdue the bulls and kill them with a single thrust of a sword. The Portuguese also have bullfights, but it is conducted on horseback by a cavaleiro. Horse and rider perform dainty manoeuvres to control the bull, which is not killed in the ring.

Modern museum

The Guggenheim Museum in the Spanish city of Bilbao is home to famous works of art. The building is made from titanium and glass.

Collecting cork

Cork is usually harvested in August. The heat makes the cork layer pull away, making it is easier to remove from the tree.

The far west of Europe

Portugal may be attached to Spain by a long border, but it has its own special character. The coasts of Portugal look out over the Atlantic. They are cool and misty in the north, creating a green landscape called the Costa Verde (Green Coast), but they are warmer and sunnier in the Algarve province of the south. The whitewashed towns of the Algarve are a popular destination for tourists. In the hills and mountains along the border with Spain are cork-oak forests. Bark is stripped off the trees to make bottle corks.

Fishing is an important industry in both Spain and Portugal. Vigo, in north-eastern Spain, is Europe's biggest fishing port, and fish plays a central role in Portuguese cooking. Bacalhau is a tangy stew made with salt cod and, in summer, the streets of Lisbon, the Portuguese capital, are scented with the smell of grilled sardines, cooked on street barbecues.

ITALY AND ITS NEIGHBOURS

Boot-shaped Italy kicks out into the Mediterranean Sea. Its streets, piazzas (squares) and monuments are full of reminders of its historic past. For centuries it was the heart of an ancient empire that stretched across Europe, and later it was home to Renaissance art and culture. Today, it is a vibrant, modern nation and a world leader in fashion and style.

Regional differences

Traditionally, Italy is divided into two – the cooler, more industrial and wealthier north, and the hotter, drier and poorer south. The capital, Rome, is in the middle. Italy also has two large islands – Sicily and Sardinia.

During medieval times, Italy was divided into numerous small, independent states, centring on magnificent cities, such as Florence, Venice and Milan, with their cathedrals, palaces and splendid collections of art. These small states were only brought together as one country in 1861.

Traditionally, Italians have identified strongly with the town or region where they were born. They saw themselves first as Genoan or Tuscan or Sicilian, and second as Italian. Each area has not only its distinctive dialect or accent, but also its own kinds of cooking, and brands of coffee and wine. Naples, for example, is famed for its pizzas, and Parma for its cured ham.

The towns and cities are very proud of their identity and history. Most towns hold a festival in the summer, when leading national or international musicians, opera singers and pop stars are invited to perform. Even small villages hold a sagra (an outdoor summer feast), where the local food speciality is served up at long trestle tables and the whole community dances to the music of a local rock band. Even on ordinary days there is a festive air in many towns in the early evening, especially in the summer, when people walk in the streets, shop, chat and drink in a café – a custom called the passeggiata.

Cars and clothes

Agriculture has always been an important industry in Italy and the country still has many farming communities. But one-third of the labour force now works in manufacturing, and Italy is known for the design flair of its commercial products. It is home to famous car manufacturers, such as Fiat and Ferrari, and fashion designers, such as Armani and Versace. However, most people work in service industries, such as banking and tourism.

Floating city

The city of Venice has more than 150 canals running through it. The waterways bustle with waterbuses, barges and gondolas. Thousands of tourists flock to the city every year.

Tomato harvest

The Italian climate is ideal for growing tomatoes. Tomatoes originated in South America and European explorers brought them to Italy in the 1500s.

In fact, Vatican City's many priceless art treasures make it one of the richest countries in the world (per m²).

The independent republic of San Marino, just 61 km², also lies within Italy. Over half its income is generated by tourism. The wealthy independent principality of Monaco (1.9 km²) lies on the Mediterranean coast just beyond the border with France. It is famed for its glamour and casinos.

Another small state south of Italy is Malta. Its two main islands lie in the middle of a channel in the Mediterranean Sea separating Italy from Africa. The Romans, Arabs, Normans, Spanish, French and English have all ruled Malta, each leaving traces in the nation's rich mix of cultures. It became an independent nation in 1964, and now seeks European Union membership.

Pasta popularity

Pasta, of course, is Italy's best-known dish. A dough made with durum-wheat flour, it comes in at least 200 different shapes and sizes. The Italians eat a great deal of pasta. It is usually served with a sauce, such as garlic fried in olive oil with chilli, or homemade tomato sauce. Every household has its own recipe for tomato sauce, cooked and bottled each summer.

Small states

Lying in the heart of Rome is Vatican City – the world's smallest independent state and headquarters of the Roman Catholic Church. Less than 0.44 km² in size, it has about 1,000 inhabitants, including the Pope (the head of the Roman Catholic Church) and contains St Peter's Basilica, the Papal Palace and a host of magnificent museums.

Religious leader

Vatican City is home to the Pope, the head of the Roman Catholic Church. Millions of pilgrims visit the Vatican every year to hear Pope John Paul II lead prayers.

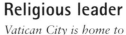

CENTRAL EUROPE

The band of countries that runs across central Europe reaches to the Baltic Sea in the north, where icy winds blow in winter. In the south lies Greece, where summers are long and hot. The landlocked countries in the middle rise up into mountains – the Carpathian and Tatra Mountains in Poland and Slovakia, and the Alps in Austria, Switzerland and Slovenia.

Goulash and Gruyère

In the flat plains of central Poland – a land of lakes and forests and medieval castles – farmers grow wheat, rye, potatoes and sugar beet. Hungary is warm enough to grow large quantities of peppers. Dried and powered, they are used to make the spice paprika, a key ingredient of the national dish goulash (a stew). In Greece, farmers grow olives, lemons, grapes and sunflowers.

Large areas of the mountains are forested, and timber is an important export of Austria and Slovenia. The valleys trap the summer warmth, where a wide range of fruit and vegetables can grow. Grapes for wine grow high in the Swiss mountains, on sheltered, south-facing terraces. Mountain farmers herd cattle and sheep. Cows' milk is used to make cheese, such as Swiss Gruyère and Emmental, which can be heated in a pot to make fondue (a melted cheese dip).

Mountain land

Over 60 per cent of Switzerland is mountainous. The Alps occupy the central and southern regions of the country and are home to many winter sports resorts.

Two paths

Events in recent history divided the countries of central Europe into two groups – communist and non-communist. After the end of World War II in 1945, communist governments took over in Poland, Hungary and Czechoslovakia, and came under the control of the Soviet Union. In 1989, as the Soviet Union collapsed, they declared their independence. Czechoslovakia split into two countries – the Czech Republic and Slovakia – in 1993.

Independence has given these countries a new opportunity to find their true identities. Each has its own distinct character and language. But they are all struggling to rebuild their economies, switching from heavy industry and mining to modern industries, making cars, domestic appliances and other consumer goods, computers and telecommunications equipment. In 1999, Poland, the Czech Republic and Hungary joined NATO (the military alliance of Western nations) and they have applied to join the

Fun on the slopes

The mountains of central Europe are home to many popular ski resorts. This young boy is travelling up a slope on a ski lift in an Austrian resort.

European Union. But they still lag behind western Europe. For example, the economy of the western European nation of France is around 30 times stronger than that of Hungary.

Austria managed to escape being taken over by the Soviet Union and has prospered as a member of the European Union. It produces iron, steel, textiles and machinery, and has more organic farmers that any other nation in Europe. Tourism is an important industry. In summer, boats take visitors down the River Danube to Vienna, the grand old capital of the Austrian empire – a city of palaces, elegant coffee houses and music. In winter, skiers and other winter-sports enthusiasts flock to the mountain ski resorts.

Switzerland is a neutral country and was not directly involved with either of the world wars, although it has a large and active citizens' army, trained and ready to defend it. Like Austria, it has plenty of ski resorts, but it also earns income from banking and from manufacturing medicines and its famous watches.

The Austrians speak German, and so too do the majority of the Swiss. But Switzerland is a multilingual land – one-fifth speak French and minorities speak Italian or a language called Romansch, which is related to Latin.

Nestling between Austria and Switzerland is the tiny German-speaking principality of Liechtenstein. It has an area of about 160 km^2, and a population of just 30,000. A small industrial country, it also earns a high income from banking.

Romany dance

There is a sizeable gypsy population in central Europe. This gypsy girl from the Czech Republic is performing a traditional folk dance.

The Balkans

The area of land from the south of Austria down to the Mediterranean Sea is known as the Balkans. For centuries it was the crossroads and the battleground between the Muslim Turks and Christian Europe. After World War II, communist leader Marshal Tito ruled over the united country of Yugoslavia (now the Union of Serbia and Montenegro). He recognized the divisions in his land and once said: "I am the leader of one country which has two alphabets, three languages, four religions and five nationalities".

Tourism trade

Croatia has managed to rebuild its tourist industry after the war in the 1990s. Its warm climate, beaches and medieval towns make it a popular destination.

Tito died in 1980, and not long after the historic stresses and strains began to show. When Serbia attempted to dominate the other republics in the early 1990s, Slovenia, Croatia and Bosnia-Herzegovina declared independence and Macedonia followed in 1991. A bloody civil war broke out, first in Croatia and then in Bosnia, between Christian Serbs and the Bosnian Muslims, before an uneasy peace was imposed in 1995 with the help of NATO forces. In 1998,

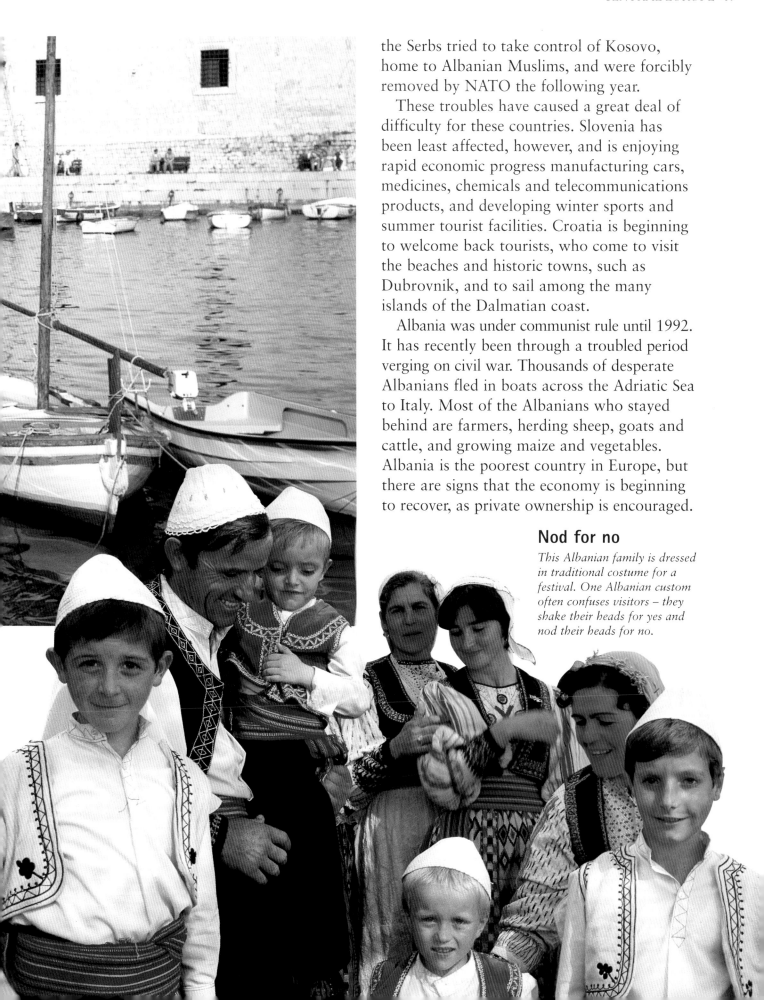

the Serbs tried to take control of Kosovo, home to Albanian Muslims, and were forcibly removed by NATO the following year.

These troubles have caused a great deal of difficulty for these countries. Slovenia has been least affected, however, and is enjoying rapid economic progress manufacturing cars, medicines, chemicals and telecommunications products, and developing winter sports and summer tourist facilities. Croatia is beginning to welcome back tourists, who come to visit the beaches and historic towns, such as Dubrovnik, and to sail among the many islands of the Dalmatian coast.

Albania was under communist rule until 1992. It has recently been through a troubled period verging on civil war. Thousands of desperate Albanians fled in boats across the Adriatic Sea to Italy. Most of the Albanians who stayed behind are farmers, herding sheep, goats and cattle, and growing maize and vegetables. Albania is the poorest country in Europe, but there are signs that the economy is beginning to recover, as private ownership is encouraged.

Nod for no

This Albanian family is dressed in traditional costume for a festival. One Albanian custom often confuses visitors – they shake their heads for yes and nod their heads for no.

The sun-drenched south

Greece, at the southern tip of central Europe, has watched nervously as its northern neighbours descended into chaos. By contrast, it has prospered as a member of the European Union and has adopted the Euro currency.

Over 2,500 years ago, Greece ruled much of the eastern Mediterranean and created the first great European civilization. The Greeks were noted as adventurous traders and sailors, and still own the fourth largest shipping fleet in the world. Numerous ships are needed to ferry goods and people around the many Greek islands in the Mediterranean – dry, rocky lumps of land dotted with whitewashed villages and crowned with the domes of ancient churches.

Greek Christians belong mainly to the Orthodox Church, which has developed along a separate path to the Roman Catholic Church since 1054. Stylized portrait paintings, called icons, depicting saints and characters from the Bible, play a central role in worship.

For thousands of years people have survived on the islands by fishing and farming. These

Painted icons
The walls of Greek Orthodox churches are often covered in iconic paintings of saints and biblical figures.

days, tourism brings in much needed extra income. They stay in small hotels and eat at local tavernas (restaurants), where traditional dishes are served, such as lamb kebabs, goats cheese, and moussaka (a dish made of minced lamb, potatoes, tomatoes and aubergines). Tourists also visit mainland Greece to see the ancient sites such as the Parthenon on the Acropolis in Athens. There are 10.5 million people living in Greece, and a third of them lives in and around Athens, the capital. The mixture of heat and dense traffic has made this one of the most polluted cities on earth, putting the ancient stone of the Acropolis under threat.

The Acropolis
The Acropolis dominates Athen's skyline. It houses the remains of Ancient Greek temples, over 2,500 years old. The columns of the Parthenon temple still stand today.

EASTERN EUROPE

Until 1989, the countries of eastern Europe were part of the Soviet Union. Now they are independent, but many of them still consider that they have more in common with Russia than with the rest of Europe. Their economies are struggling to adapt after years of Soviet rule and many countries in the region face an uncertain future.

Agriculture and industry

The Ukraine is one of Europe's largest countries. On its wide, grassy plains, farmers grow wheat, barley, sugar beet and cotton, and raise cattle and pigs. Coal is mined in large quantities in the Donets Basin in eastern Ukraine, fuelling industries that make steel, machinery and ships. Factories also produce chemicals and processed food. To the south lie the sunny coasts of the Black Sea, and the large, diamond-shaped peninsula called the Crimea, which has a number of popular beach resorts. Over two-thirds of the population live in cities. Like many of the towns and cities of the old Soviet empire, they are dominated by large apartment blocks and offices. Russian was widely spoken during the Soviet era, but Ukrainian became the official language again in 1991.

Farm work

Although farm production is largely mechanised, some farmers still take their produce to market in horse-drawn carts.

Nuclear legacy

The Ukraine is haunted by a tragic legacy of Soviet rule. In 1986, a nuclear power plant at Chernobyl, to the north of the city of Kiev, exploded, spilling radioactive waste into the air and poisoning a vast area of farmland. It killed 31 people immediately, but some 25,000 people have since died from illnesses such as cancer, caused by the radioactive fallout. It is the worst nuclear accident on record.

Dracula and roses

Romania was ruled for 25 years by a communist dictator called Nicolae Ceausescu. One of his most unpopular policies was to create huge farms by destroying 7,000 villages. In 1989, he was overthrown in a rebellion and executed. The country has been trying to recover from these events by developing its industries. The Black Sea coast is popular in the summer. Walkers can explore the beautiful Carpathian Mountains and the Transylvania Alps – the home, according to legends, of vampires. Bran Castle is said to be the castle of the original Count Dracula. Romania also has winter sports resorts, such as Poiana Brasov in Transylvania.

About two per cent of Romanians are gypsies. No-one is quite sure where they came from originally, but they have lived in Romania for over 1,000 years, and have spread out to many other parts of Europe. Gypsies speak a language called Romany, but confusingly, the name has nothing to do with Romania. They are the source of much of the lively violin music and dance traditions of eastern Europe. Despite this, they have suffered a long history of persecution and discrimination, which became more acute after the collapse of communism.

Bulgaria produces grain, fruit and a range of vegetables on a fertile plain that stretches southwards from the River Danube to the Balkan Mountains in the middle of the country. Over 20 per cent of the population earn their income from farming – a very high proportion by European standards. Many of them grow roses, to make essence of rose, which is used in the perfume industry. Colossal amounts of the flowers are needed – it takes over 3,000 kg of rose petals to make one litre of rose oil.

Uncertain future

Moldova has rich, dark soil which is the basis of its agricultural industry, producing fruit such as apples and grapes, as well as nuts and honey. Over half the population lives and works on farms, and much of the food is sent to factories in the food-processing industry. Most of the people are Moldovans, who are close relations to Romanians, but there are large minorities of Ukrainians and Russians.

Of all the countries of eastern Europe, Moldova has suffered the most in the recent political changes, and misses the support once given to it by the Soviet Union. Its industries have collapsed and unemployment is soaring.

Dracula's castle

Despite popular myth, Bran Castle has no historic links with Vlad Tepes, the cruel medieval prince on whom writer Bram Stoker based his Dracula story. However, its fairytale turrets make it a popular tourist attraction.

RUSSIA

Russia is the largest country in the world – it stretches a third of the way around the globe. A quarter of the country lies north of the Arctic Circle, and long, bitterly cold winters are part of Russian life. It takes seven days to cross Russia on the Trans-Siberian Railway, which runs from the capital Moscow to Vladivostok on the Pacific coast.

About a fifth of Russia is in Europe and the rest is in Asia. The dividing line is the Ural Mountains. These form a band running north to south some 2,000 km east of Russia's capital, Moscow. There is good farmland in European Russia, especially in the warmer, southern regions, which reach down to the Black Sea. Large, government-owned farms grow grain and fruit and raise cattle. In the south, farmers grow peaches and oranges.

Communist rule

For over 70 years during the 20th century, Russia was ruled by a communist government, and was at the head of a large country called the Soviet Union. The government owned all land, buildings, farms and factories on behalf of all the people. The Soviet government exerted strict control over the people, limiting what they could say and do, as well as where they could go.

For many years, the Soviet Union was involved in a 'Cold War' with Western nations led by the USA. The West feared communism, and the two sides developed nuclear weapons arsenals in case the other side attacked. This was a huge drain on Soviet resources. In addition, the lack of industrial competition in the Soviet Union had led to an over-bureaucratic and inefficient system, and the economy of the country began to crumble during the 1980s.

Wheat harvest

Despite its size, much of Russia lacks proper soils and climates for agriculture – it is either too cold or too dry. The fertile land of western Russia is used to grow crops and raise livestock.

The Kremlin

The Kremlin occupies a triangular plot of land in Russia's capital, Moscow. It was the government's power base during the Soviet years.

In 1991, the communist government collapsed and the Soviet Union broke up. Many satellite states, such as Kazahkstan, Azerbaijan and Armenia, demanded independence from Moscow. With Russia, they formed a new group of 12 countries called the Commonwealth of Independent States (CIS). Russia itself is also called the Russian Federation and includes 21 self-governing member republics. Some of these have expressed a desire to be free of Russian control – including the southern republic of Chechnya, where war has raged.

Northern people

The Dolgan people originate in northern Russia and traditionally lived by fishing and hunting reindeer. Under Soviet rule, they were forced to work on collective farms.

New opportunities

Since 1991, Russia has been struggling to modernize its economy, and to move from a communist system to a market economy, where companies compete for business. This meant switching from the old state-run heavy industries, producing coal, steel, ships, machinery and chemicals, to producing things to export to the rest of the world, such as electrical equipment, cameras and cars. Russia has had some difficult times adjusting, but there are signs that private enterprise is helping the economy to grow again.

In general, Russians have welcomed the changes. Under the communist regime, shops had little in them, and goods were generally of low quality. Now Russians can buy imported goods from all over the world. But the market economy has brought problems.

Under the Soviet regime there was no unemployment – now a sizeable part of the workforce is without a job. In addition, the reliable welfare and healthcare systems have withered away.

Russia has vast natural resources – plenty of oil and natural gas, coal, timber and metals. Many of these come from the tundra and forests of Siberia in central Russia, and are processed by industrial cities such as Omsk and Krasnoyarsk, which lie on the route of the Trans-Siberian Railway.

Onion domes

Russian churches are famous for their onion-shaped domes. They are painted in bright colours or covered in glittering gold leaf and give Russian cities unique skylines. These star-covered blue domes top the Yuzier Monastery in Moscow.

A mixture of peoples

Russia contains over 100 different peoples.
Russians make up over 80 per cent of the
population, but there are also Tartars,
Chuvash and Bashkir in western (European)
Russia, Nenets in the far north and Yakuts in
Siberia, to name but a few. Each has their
own traditions and identity. Under the
communists, thousands of people were moved
around the country, so the populations have
become very mixed.

Under communism, religion was discouraged,
but today people are allowed to worship freely.
The majority of worshippers are Russian
Orthodox Christians, but a sizeable minority
are Muslims, especially in the south.

The Russian cities of St Petersburg and
Moscow rival each other as cultural centres.
They have fine churches, palaces, ballet
schools, art museums, and a great
tradition of music and literature.

Cold north

*In northern Siberia, the winters are very cold, with
temperatures plummeting to -40°C. Hardy reindeer
are used to pull sleighs along the icy roads.*

Orthodox Church

*Many people in Russia
belong to the Russian
Orthodox Church, a branch
of Christianity. During the
Soviet era, religion was
oppressed, but people now
have religious freedom.*

ALBANIA

Capital
Tirana
Area
28,748 km²
Population
3,113,000
Population density
132 per km²
Life expectancy
69 (m); 75 (f)
Religions
Christianity, Islam
Languages
Albanian (dialects: Gheg in north, Tosk in south)
Adult literacy rate
95 per cent
Currency
lek

 ANDORRA

Capital
Andorra la Vella
Area
468 km²
Population
80,000
Population density
158 per km²
Life expectancy
79 (m); 79 (f)
Religion
Christianity
Languages
Catalan, French, Spanish
Adult literacy rate
99 per cent
Currency
euro

 AUSTRIA

Capital
Vienna
Area
83,858 km²
Population
8,177,000
Population density
96 per km²
Life expectancy
73 (m); 80 (f)
Religion
Christianity
Language
German
Adult literacy rate
99 per cent
Currency
euro

 BELARUS

Capital
Minsk
Area
207,595 km²
Population
10,159,000
Population density
49 per km²
Life expectancy
62 (m); 74 (f)
Religion
Christianity
Languages
Belarussian, Russian
Adult literacy rate
98 per cent
Currency
Belarussian rouble

 BELGIUM

Capital
Brussels
Area
30,528 km²
Population
10,152,000
Population density
334 per km²
Life expectancy
72 (m); 79 (f)
Religion
Christianity
Languages
Flemish, French, German
Adult literacy rate
99 per cent
Currency
euro

 BOSNIA AND HERZEGOVINA

Capital
Sarajevo
Area
51,129 km²
Population
3,839,000
Population density
82 per km²
Life expectancy
69 (m); 75 (f)
Religions
Islam, Christianity
Languages
Serbo-Croat (Muslims and Croats use Roman script; Serbs use Cyrillic)
Adult literacy rate
93 per cent
Currency
marka

BULGARIA

Capital
Sofia
Area
110,994 km²
Population
8,208,000
Population density
74 per km²
Life expectancy
67 (m); 74 (f)
Religions
Christianity, Islam
Languages
Bulgarian, Turkish
Adult literacy rate
92 per cent
Currency
lev

 CROATIA

Capital
Zagreb
Area
56,610 km²
Population
4,554,000
Population density
81 per km²
Life expectancy
68 (m); 76 (f)
Religion
Christianity
Language
Serbo-Croat (Roman script)
Adult literacy rate
93 per cent
Currency
kuna

 CZECH REPUBLIC

Capital
Prague
Area
78,864 km²
Population
10,283,000
Population density
130 per km²
Life expectancy
70 (m); 77 (f)
Religion
Christianity
Languages
Czech, German and others
Adult literacy rate
99 per cent
Currency
Czech koruna

 DENMARK

Capital
Copenhagen
Area
43,094 km²
Population
5,327,000
Population density
123 per km²
Life expectancy
72 (m); 77 (f)
Religion
Christianity
Language
Danish
Adult literacy rate
99 per cent
Currency
Danish krone

 ESTONIA

Capital
Tallinn
Area
45,227 km²
Population
1,370,500
Population density
32 per km²
Life expectancy
62 (m); 73 (f)
Religion
Christianity
Languages
Estonian, Russian
Adult literacy rate
99 per cent
Currency
kroon

 FINLAND

Capital
Helsinki
Area
338,144 km²
Population
5,165,000
Population density
15 per km²
Life expectancy
72 (m); 80 (f)
Religion
Christianity
Languages
Finnish, Swedish, Lapp
Adult literacy rate
99 per cent
Currency
euro

FRANCE

Capital
Paris
Area
543,965 km²
Population
59,099,000
Population density
108 per km²
Life expectancy
73 (m); 81 (f)
Religion
Christianity
Languages
French, Breton, Basque and several regional dialects
Adult literacy rate
95 per cent
Currency
euro

 GERMANY

Capital
Berlin
Area
356,974 km²
Population
82,087,000
Population density
230 per km²
Life expectancy
72 (m); 79 (f)
Religion
Christianity
Language
German
Adult literacy rate
99 per cent
Currency
euro

 **GREECE**

Capital
Athens
Area
131,957 km²
Population
10,626,000
Population density
80 per km²
Life expectancy
75 (m); 80 (f)
Religion
Christianity
Language
Greek (Demotiki, or modern Greek)
Adult literacy rate
95 per cent
Currency
euro

French food

France has a reputation for its fine cuisine. Stores, big and small, stock fine patés, cheeses and patisserie (bread and cakes).

 HUNGARY

Capital
Budapest
Area
93,030 km²
Population
10,068,000
Population density
109 per km²
Life expectancy
65 (m); 74 (f)
Religion
Christianity
Language
Hungarian
Adult literacy rate
99 per cent
Currency
forint

Dressing up

Greece has many national traditions and every region has its own unique one as well.

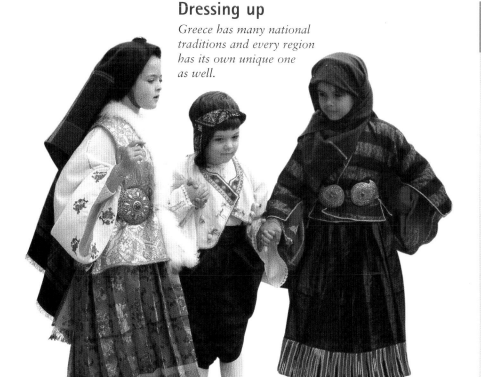

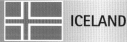

ICELAND

Capital
Reykjavik
Area
103,000 km²
Population
279,000
Population density
3 per km²
Life expectancy
76 (m); 80 (f)
Religion
Christianity
Language
Icelandic
Adult literacy rate
99 per cent
Currency
Icelandic króna

IRELAND

Capital
Dublin
Area
70,285 km²
Population
3,745,000
Population density
53 per km²
Life expectancy
72 (m); 78 (f)
Religion
Christianity
Languages
Irish, English
Adult literacy rate
99 per cent
Currency
euro

ITALY

Capital
Rome
Area
301,323 km²
Population
57,343,000
Population density
191 per km²
Life expectancy
74 (m); 80 (f)
Religion
Christianity
Languages
Italian, German, French, others
Adult literacy rate
97 per cent
Currency
euro

LATVIA

Capital
Riga
Area
64,589 km²
Population
2,432,000
Population density
38 per km²
Life expectancy
60 (m); 73 (f)
Religion
Christianity
Languages
Latvian, Russian
Adult literacy rate
98 per cent
Currency
lats

LIECHTENSTEIN

Capital
Vaduz
Area
160 km²
Population
32,000
Population density
200 per km²
Life expectancy
66 (m); 73 (f)
Religion
Christianity
Language
German (Alemannic dialect)
Adult literacy rate
95 per cent
Currency
Swiss franc

 LITHUANIA

Capital
Vilnius
Area
65,300 km²
Population
3,699,000
Population density
57 per km²
Life expectancy
63 (m); 75 (f)
Religion
Christianity
Languages
Lithuanian, Russian, Polish
Adult literacy rate
98 per cent
Currency
litas

 LUXEMBOURG

Capital
Luxembourg
Area
2,587 km²
Population
429,000
Population density
166 per km²
Life expectancy
70 (m); 77 (f)
Religion
Christianity
Languages
Letzeburghish (German-
Moselle-Frankish dialect),
French, German
Adult literacy rate
99 per cent
Currency
euro

 **MACEDONIA**

Capital
Skopje
Area
25,713 km²
Population
2,011,000
Population density
78 per km²
Life expectancy
69 (m); 73 (f)
Religions
Christianity, Islam
Languages
Macedonian, Albanian, Serbo-
Croat (Cyrillic script)
Adult literacy rate
93 per cent
Currency
Macedonian denar

 MALTA

Capital
Valletta
Area
316 km²
Population
386,000
Population density
1,203 per km²
Life expectancy
75 (m); 79 (f)
Religion
Christianity
Languages
Maltese, English, Italian
Adult literacy rate
88 per cent
Currency
Maltese lira

 MOLDOVA

Capital
Chisinau
Area
33,700 km²
Population
4,380,000
Population density
108 per km²
Life expectancy
62 (m); 69 (f)
Religion
Christianity
Languages
Moldovan, Russian
Adult literacy rate
96 per cent
Currency
Moldovan leu

MONACO

Capital
Monaco-Ville
Area
1.95 km²
Population
33,000
Population density
16,410 per km²
Life expectancy
78 (m); 78 (f)
Religion
Christianity
Languages
French, Monegasque, Italian, English
Adult literacy rate
99 per cent
Currency
euro

NETHERLANDS

Capital
Amsterdam (government at The Hague)
Area
33,939 km²
Population
15,810,000
Population density
463 per km²
Life expectancy
74 (m); 80 (f)
Religion
Christianity
Language
Dutch
Adult literacy rate
99 per cent
Currency
euro

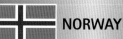

NORWAY

Capital
Oslo
Area
323,877 km²
Population
4,462,000
Population density
14 per km²
Life expectancy
74 (m); 80 (f)
Religion
Christianity
Languages
Norwegian, Lapp
Adult literacy rate
99 per cent
Currency
Norwegian krone

Waterways

Amsterdam, the capital city of the Netherlands in northern Europe, has 160 canals running through it, and over 1,200 bridges.

POLAND

Capital
Warsaw
Area
312,685 km²
Population
38,654,000
Population density
124 per km²
Life expectancy
67 (m); 76 (f)
Religion
Christianity
Languages
Polish, German
Adult literacy rate
99 per cent
Currency
zloty

PORTUGAL

Capital
Lisbon
Area
92,270 km²
Population
9,989,000
Population density
108 per km²
Life expectancy
71 (m); 78 (f)
Religion
Christianity
Language
Portuguese
Adult literacy rate
85 per cent
Currency
euro

 ROMANIA

Capital
Bucharest
Area
238,391 km²
Population
22,458,000
Population density
94 per km²
Life expectancy
65 (m); 73 (f)
Religion
Christianity
Languages
Romanian, Hungarian,
German and others
Adult literacy rate
97 per cent
Currency
Romanian leu

 RUSSIA

Capital
Moscow
Area
17,075,400 km²
Population
145,943,000
Population density
9 per km²
Life expectancy
58 (m); 71 (f)
Religions
Christianity, Islam, Judaism
Languages
Russian, Tatar, Yakut,
Chuvash, Bashkir and others
Adult literacy rate
99 per cent
Currency
rouble

 SAN MARINO

Capital
San Marino
Area
61 km²
Population
26,000
Population density
492 per km²
Life expectancy
73 (m); 79 (f)
Religion
Christianity
Language
Italian
Adult literacy rate
98 per cent
Currency
euro

 SLOVAKIA

Capital
Bratislava
Area
49,036 km²
Population
5,395,000
Population density
110 per km²
Life expectancy
68 (m); 76 (f)
Religion
Christianity
Languages
Slovak, Hungarian, Czech and
others
Adult literacy rate
93 per cent
Currency
Slovak koruna

 SLOVENIA

Capital
Ljubljana
Area
20,253 km²
Population
1,986,000
Population density
98 per km²
Life expectancy
70 (m); 77 (f)
Religion
Christianity
Languages
Slovene, Serbo-Croat (Roman
script), Hungarian, Italian
Adult literacy rate
99 per cent
Currency
tolar

SPAIN

Capital
Madrid
Area
504,782 km²
Population
39,418,000
Population density
78 per km²
Life expectancy
73 (m); 80 (f)
Religion
Christianity
Languages
Spanish (Castilian), Catalan, Galician, Basque
Adult literacy rate
96 per cent
Currency
euro

Fair frills

This man is wearing traditional costume for a fair in Andalucia in Spain. This region is home to flamenco music and dance.

 SWEDEN

Capital
Stockholm
Area
449,964 km²
Population
8,861,000
Population density
20 per km²
Life expectancy
76 (m); 81 (f)
Religion
Christianity
Languages
Swedish, Finnish, Lapp
Adult literacy rate
99 per cent
Currency
Swedish krona

 SWITZERLAND

Capital
Berne (Bern)
Area
41,284 km²
Population
7,140,000
Population density
172 per km²
Life expectancy
75 (m); 82 (f)
Religion
Christianity
Languages
German, French, Italian, Romansch and others
Adult literacy rate
99 per cent
Currency
Swiss franc

UKRAINE

Capital
Kiev
Area
603,700 km²
Population
50,106,000
Population density
84 per km²
Life expectancy
62 (m); 73 (f)
Religion
Christianity
Languages
Ukrainian, Russian, Romanian, Hungarian, Polish
Adult literacy rate
96 per cent
Currency
hryvnya

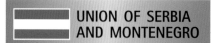 **UNION OF SERBIA AND MONTENEGRO**

Capital
Belgrade
Area
102,173 km²
Population
10,637,000
Population density
104 per km²
Life expectancy
68 (m); 74 (f)
Religions
Christianity, Islam
Language
Serbo-Croat (Cyrillic script)
Adult literacy rate
89 per cent
Currency
Yugoslav new dinar

 **UNITED KINGDOM**

Capital
London
Area
241,752 km²
Population
59,200,000
Population density
245 per km²
Life expectancy
74 (m); 79 (f)
Religion
Christianity
Languages
English, Welsh
Adult literacy rate
99 per cent
Currency
pound sterling

 VATICAN CITY

Area
0.44 km²
Population
About 1,000
Population density
1,977 per km²
Life expectancy
74 (m); 80 (f)
Religion
Christianity
Languages
Italian, Latin
Adult literacy rate
100 per cent
Currency
euro

Rural appeal

Although most people in the United Kindom live in towns and cities, there are also large areas of beautiful, green countryside such as Somerset and Dorest.

The United States of America

Canada

Mexico

The Caribbean

Central America

NORTH AMERICA

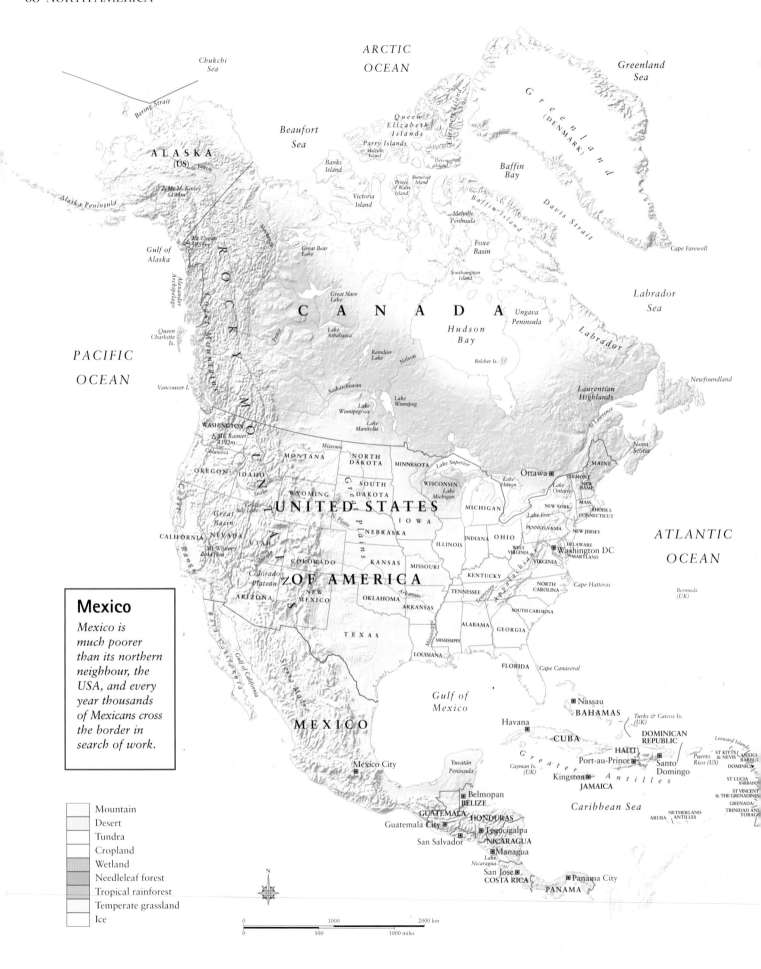

ARCTIC
OCEAN

Chukchi
Sea

Greenland
Sea

Beaufort
Sea

Queen
Elizabeth
Islands

Melville
Island

Ellesmere Island

ALASKA
(US)
Yukon

G
r
e
e
n
l
a
n
d
(DENMARK)

Banks
Island

Prince
of Wales
Island

Somerset
Island

Devon
Island

Baffin
Bay

△ *Mt McKinley*
6194m

Victoria
Island

Davis Strait

Alaska Peninsula

Mackenzie

Melville
Peninsula

Baffin Island

Cape Farewell

△ *Mt Logan*
5959m

Gulf of
Alaska

R
O
C
K
Y

Great Bear
Lake

Foxe
Basin

Alexander
Archipelago

Southampton
Island

Labrador
Sea

Queen
Charlotte
Is.

C
o
a
s
t

M
o
u
n
t
a
i
n
s

Peace

Great Slave
Lake

C A N A D A

Hudson
Bay

Ungava
Peninsula

Labrador

PACIFIC

OCEAN

M
O
U
N
T

Vancouver I.

Reindeer
Lake

Nelson

Belcher Is.

Laurentian
Highlands

Newfoundland

Saskatchewan

Lake
Athabasca

Lake
Winnipegosis

Lake
Winnipeg

St Lawrence

WASHINGTON
△ *Mt Rainier*
4392m

A
I
N
S

Lake
Manitoba

Nova
Scotia

Columbia

OREGON

IDAHO

Snake

MONTANA

Missouri

NORTH
DAKOTA

MINNESOTA

Lake Superior

Ottawa ■

MAINE

△ *Mt Logan*

WYOMING

Great
Basin

Great
Salt Lake

N. Platte

SOUTH
DAKOTA

WISCONSIN
Lake
Michigan

Lake
Huron

VERMONT
NEW
HAMP.

Lake
Ontario

CALIFORNIA

NEVADA
△ *Mt Whitney*
4418m

UTAH

Colorado

COLORADO

G
r
e
a
t

P
l
a
i
n
s

IOWA

NEBRASKA

MICHIGAN

NEW YORK

MASS.
RHODE I.
CONNECTICUT

UNITED STATES

ILLINOIS

INDIANA

OHIO

PENNSYLVANIA

NEW JERSEY

DELAWARE
MARYLAND

ATLANTIC

OCEAN

C
o
a
s
t

R
a
n
g
e
s

Colorado
Plateau

ARIZONA

Z OF AMERICA

NEW
MEXICO

KANSAS

OKLAHOMA

Arkansas

MISSOURI

KENTUCKY

WEST
VIRGINIA

VIRGINIA

■ Washington DC

Appalachian

Tennessee

NORTH
CAROLINA

Cape Hatteras

Bermuda
(UK)

S
i
e
r
r
a

M
a
d
r
e

Gulf of California

Baja California

TEXAS

ARKANSAS

Mississippi

MISSISSIPPI

TENNESSEE

ALABAMA

GEORGIA

SOUTH
CAROLINA

LOUISIANA

FLORIDA

Cape Canaveral

MEXICO

■ Nassau

Turks & Caicos Is.
(UK)

Gulf of
Mexico

Havana ■

BAHAMAS

Leeward Islands

■ Mexico City

Yucatán
Peninsula

Cayman Is.
(UK)

CUBA

HAITI

G
r
e
a
t
e
r

DOMINICAN
REPUBLIC

Port-au-Prince ■

Kingston ■

A
n
t
i
l
l
e
s

■ Santo
Domingo

Puerto
Rico (US)

ST KITTS
& NEVIS

ANTIGUA
BARBUDA

DOMINICA

JAMAICA

ST LUCIA
BARBADOS

ST VINCENT
& THE GRENADINES

GRENADA

■ Belmopan

Caribbean Sea

NETHERLAND
ANTILLES

TRINIDAD AND
TOBAGO

BELIZE

GUATEMALA

HONDURAS

ARUBA

NETHERLAND
ANTILLES

Guatemala City ■

■ Tegucigalpa

San Salvador ■

NICARAGUA

■ Managua

Lake
Nicaragua

San Jose ■
COSTA RICA

■ Panama City

PANAMA

Mexico

Mexico is much poorer than its northern neighbour, the USA, and every year thousands of Mexicans cross the border in search of work.

	Mountain
	Desert
	Tundra
	Cropland
	Wetland
	Needleleaf forest
	Tropical rainforest
	Temperate grassland
	Ice

N

0	1000	2000 km
0	500	1000 miles

THE UNITED STATES OF AMERICA

Stretching across the North American continent, the United States of America (USA) is the world's leading power. A land of diverse geography and climates, it is divided into 50 states and is a melting pot of people and cultures. It is largely populated by descendants of immigrants, who came in the past seeking a new life in the 'land of opportunity'.

North America was home to native populations for thousands of years before the first European explorers arrived in the 15th century. During the 15th and 16th centuries, however, much of the native Americans' land was taken over by colonies of settlers from Britain, France and Spain. During the War of Independence in the 18th century, 13 colonies won freedom from British rule and the USA was born. Over time the new nation expanded west, until it stretched from the Atlantic coast in the east to the coast of the Pacific Ocean in the west. Its vast natural resources and political stability has enabled the USA to become the most powerful nation in the world, exerting economic, political and cultural influences on other countries.

The White House

The US government is based in Washington DC. It is headed by the president who lives in the White House.

Geographical diversity

The USA is a land of immense variety. It is the fourth largest country in the world (after Russia, Canada and China), with an area of over nine million km².

In the far north is the state of Alaska. It was bought from Russia in 1867 and became a state in 1959. Alaska borders Canada and is not connected by land to the rest of the USA.

Although a huge state, Alaska has a tiny population of just 627,000. However, it is home to a huge array of wildlife, including bears, moose and bald eagles. It has a dramatic landscape of glaciers and fjords and has vast natural reserves of oil and gas.

The Atlantic coast is home to some of the oldest US cities, such as Boston, New York City and Philadelphia. The capital, Washington DC, is also located in eastern USA, about midway between north and south.

In the central north-east of the country lie the Great Lakes (Superior, Michigan, Huron, Erie and Ontario), which occupy an area larger than most European countries.

Much of the centre of the USA is made up of vast plains, covered with wheatfields and cattle ranches. The mighty Mississippi, Missouri and Ohio rivers cut across the land. Further west, on the Great Plains, are the country's main grazing areas.

Mountain high

Mount Shuksan is part of the North Cascades mountain range in the state of Washington, in north-western USA. It towers 2,173 m above sea level and is a popular skiing resort.

Rocky landscape

The Grand Canyon is located in the state of Arizona. This magnificent land feature has been eroded by the Colorado river over the last five million years.

This is where America's famous cowboys once herded their cattle.

The snow-capped Rocky Mountains separate the Great Plains from the arid lands and deserts of the west coast. The state of California and its major cities of San Francisco and Los Angeles lie on the west coast. Hollywood in Los Angeles is home to the movie industry – the hot, sunny climate has attracted movie-makers since the early days of cinema. But this part of the USA is prone to earthquakes and children have drills at school to practise what emergency measures to take if an earthquake strikes.

The south-east has a hot, humid climate with areas of grassland and subtropical swampland in the state of Florida. The south-east coast is vulnerable to hurricanes in summer. These build up over the Atlantic Ocean and batter coastal towns.

Besides the Everglades National Park, Florida's tourist attractions include Disney World and the John F Kennedy Space Center at Cape Canaveral.

The USA also includes Hawaii, a group of volcanic tropical islands in the middle of the Pacific Ocean, over 3,700 km from the west coast of mainland USA. Hawaii has a hot climate and is a popular tourist destination. It has been under US rule since 1898, but it only became a state in 1959.

The people of the USA

There are 281 million people in the USA. Most come from families whose origins are elsewhere in the world, and who arrived as immigrants at some point in the last four centuries.

The original inhabitants of North America are called native Americans. They formed hundreds of groups, such as the Powhatan on the east coast, the Cherokee in the Appalachian Mountains, the Navajo in the arid lands of the south-west and the Sioux in the Great Plains. Europeans began to settle in their lands from the early 1600s – the British in the east, and the Spanish in the south and south-west. As the Europeans spread out over the continent during the next 250 years, many of the native Americans died through warfare and from exposure to new diseases. The remainder were forced to live in reservations – pockets of land put aside for them.

There are now only around two million native Americans, living mainly in the south-west. They are proud of their ancient traditions, and determined to preserve them through folk tales, festivals, art, music and dancing.

Black Americans

In the 17th, 18th and 19th centuries, the European settlers developed huge plantations in south-eastern USA to grow crops such as tobacco and cotton. They needed plenty of labour to work in the fields, so they bought slaves, who were shipped across the Atlantic from western Africa. About a million slaves in total were transported over three centuries.

Slavery was one of the main issues that divided the northern and the southern states and caused the Civil War that tore the USA apart between 1861 and 1865. Slavery was abolished after the war, and African-Americans became free, with the same rights as any other Americans, although racial segregation continued in southern states. But all over the country, African-Americans were still 'locked' into a world of poverty and prejudice, which made it very difficult for them to prosper. In the 1950s and 1960s, civil rights campaigners protested against segregation and discrimination, and did much to increase racial equality. Today, African-Americans make up 12 per cent of the US population.

Navajo celebration

This boy belongs to the Navajo people. He is wearing a traditional feather headdress, which is only worn for special tribal events, such as powwows (gatherings with other tribes).

Sunday service

An African-American family attends Sunday service in a church in Miami, Florida.

The melting pot

During the 19th and early 20th centuries, huge numbers of immigrants arrived in the USA from Italy, Ireland, Germany, Scandinavia and Russia. They were escaping persecution or seeking a better life. Thousands of Chinese workers were brought across the Pacific Ocean to help build the railways, and many stayed on. Other immigrants came from Japan, the Philippines and the South Pacific Islands, from Mexico and Central and South America. Often they were trying to escape poverty and unemployment in their own countries, or religious and political persecution.

Chinese New Year

This young Chinese-American girl has dressed up in traditional Chinese clothes to take part in a Chinese New Year parade in Los Angeles, California.

Mixed class

American school children learn about the cultures and traditions of their classmates' families. All schools in the country also proudly display the US flag.

The USA was championed as the 'Land of the Free' and, provided that these newcomers were loyal to the country and respected its traditions, they were generally free to create their own communities and practise their own religions.

Today, the Irish community in New York City celebrates St Patrick's Day with a big parade. New York City is also home to large Jewish and Italian communities. Chinese New Year is celebrated in the Chinatown districts of San Francisco and other large cities and a German community in Frankenmuth, Michigan, has created a Bavarian-style town, complete with a traditional annual German beer festival. The Amish, a Protestant Christian sect originally from Switzerland,

France and Germany, have large communities in Pennsylvania where they farm without the help of any machines. The Mormons, who follow their own form of Christianity and rules of conduct, dominate the state of Utah, and its capital, Salt Lake City.

Team mates

The USA has a troubled history of racial segregation and discrimination, but it now has a more equal society and children of all races play together.

Cars play a key role in American life. It was in the USA in 1913 that the Ford Company first started mass-producing cheaper cars that ordinary people could afford, and today most families own at least one car.

In some states, people can learn to drive a car at the age of 15 and drive themselves to school. But most children get to school on traditional yellow school buses. These buses are given top priority on the streets – no car can pass them when they stop to pick up or drop off children.

Building blocks

New York City, like other US cities, is made up of grid-like blocks. It is famous for its skyline, with towering skyscrapers, such as the Empire State building.

Shopping heaven

Shopping malls, such as the Mall of America in Minneapolis, are located on the outskirts of towns, and are full of chain stores and fast-food restaurants.

Life in the USA

American culture is well-known throughout the world thanks to the international popularity of US television programmes and Hollywood films. It has also influenced other countries' cultures. For instance, the USA invented the casual-wear look of T-shirts, jeans, trainers and baseball caps. They invented supermarkets, and fast-food restaurants selling hotdogs, hamburgers and pizza.

Some 77 per cent of Americans live in towns and cities. Most of these are laid out in a grid pattern of neatly criss-crossing streets, forming blocks filled with buildings. The centre of a city, the 'downtown' area, is often a cluster of high-rise modern buildings, with offices, shops and apartment blocks. Further out, in the suburbs, streets are lined with homes, often fronted by open lawns and with fenced yards (gardens) to the rear. Many people do their shopping at out of town commercial centres, where there are huge shopping malls and plenty of parking space.

Off to school

Yellow school buses travel from block to block picking up and dropping off children. Most people are educated to the age of 18, when they graduate from high school.

Part of the American dream is to make life easier, more efficient, comfortable and enjoyable. The Americans were the first to fill their homes with electronic gadgets, such as telephones, refrigerators, televisions, air-conditioning units, microwave ovens and computers. However, prosperity has brought its own problems.

The popularity of fast and convenience foods, combined with dependence on cars and gadgets, has had an impact on people's health. Many Americans are not eating a nutritious, balanced diet or doing enough exercise and an estimated 18 per cent of the population are obese (dangerously overweight).

American English

The Americans are united by lifestyle, but also by language. Almost everyone speaks English, the country's official language. But the gradual increase in the 'Hispanic' population (immigrants from Mexico, Central and South America, the Dominican Republic, Puerto Rico and Cuba) makes Spanish the second most-spoken language. Some ten per cent of the population speak Spanish as their first language. Over 30 other languages are also spoken as first languages in the USA.

Childhood

Like other children around the world, Americans are encouraged from early childhood to develop their talents, be they in sports, music or acting. Parents encourage their children to succeed at school and to have as much fun as possible. Special television programmes are made for children – such as the internationally successful *Sesame Street*, and restaurants often give children crayons and place mats to colour in. The USA is also the birthplace of the theme park – Disneyland in California was the first, created in 1955. There are now many others, and every year they add new, more exciting and ingenious attractions and rides.

Holidays

Christmas is the biggest public holiday in the USA. Friends exchange Christmas cards, often including photographs of their family. The shops are full of decorations, and television commercials take on a seasonal note, encouraging customers to spend ever more on presents.

Families gather to eat and drink and exchange gifts and, for many people in the northern USA, Christmas is also a time of snow for tobogganing and ice-skating.

Almost as important – and more typically American – is Thanksgiving Day. This national holiday takes place on the last Thursday in November, and marks the feast held in 1621 by the 'Pilgrim Fathers' of the Plymouth Colony – some of the earliest European settlers in the USA – to celebrate the successful completion of their first year. The Thanksgiving meal traditionally consists of all-American food, such as turkey with cranberry sauce, and pumpkin pie.

Another big celebration is held on 4 July – Independence Day. It is a public holiday, and firework displays are held all over the country to commemorate the end of British rule and the founding of the US nation.

Cartoon capers

Families flock to Disneyland in California and Disney World in Florida not only for the fun rides, but to meet Disney cartoon characters, such as Minnie Mouse.

Americans tend to take their holidays in the USA rather than travelling abroad – only a small percentage actually have a passport, and many have little knowledge of the rest of the world. They do, however, have an extraordinary range of destinations to go to on their doorstep, from the warm beaches of Florida to the mountains and forests of the Rockies, and from the historic old towns like Williamsburg in Virginia to the bright-lights, gambling halls and fantasy hotels of Las Vegas.

Many choose to spend their holidays in the 'great outdoors', taking their tents or camper vans to the countryside. The National Parks preserve hundreds of the most beautiful parts of the North American landscape.

Many children go off to summer camp during the long summer holidays. As well as doing sports and learning handicrafts, camps offer a wide range of activities and some include courses in computers, photography, film-making and adventure training.

Summer camp

Summer camp is a great place to learn new skills, have fun and make new friends. These children are learning about the environment.

Great outdoors

The varied landscape of the USA is popular with campers and hikers. This family is exploring the mountains of northern California.

Sport

When they are not on holiday, Americans make full use of their precious leisure time. Many of them participate in sports, such as tennis, swimming, running, golf, football, volleyball and athletics. The great national games are baseball, basketball, ice hockey, and American football, in which players wear helmets and bulky shoulder and thigh pads to prevent injury. All these various games are played by professionals to a high standard in national leagues. Thousands attend matches and games in huge arenas and stadiums, and millions tune in to big games on television. The annual American football Superbowl often attracts the biggest television audience of the year. Baseball's leading tournament, played at the end of the season, is called the World Series.

Tackling game

American football developed from the English game of rugby. Despite its name, the foot hardly ever touches the ball. Players wear helmets and shields to protect them during tackles.

Leading sports players such as the tennis player Jennifer Capriati and the golfer Tiger Woods are great celebrities in the USA, and it is the ambition of many children to achieve similar success one day. They start in school or local teams, then work their way up through state competitions to national championships.

Net gains

Tennis stars like Jennifer Capriati can earn millions of dollars competing in major Grand Slam tennis tournaments.

Many top sports players, particularly in athletics and American football, also get special, intensive training at college (university) level.

As a result of this great interest in sport, and the high standards of training and of sports facilities, the USA is usually the leading medal winner at the Olympic Games. In fact, the country has won twice as many medals as any other country since the modern games began. It has numerous outstanding champions and record-beaters, such as the athletes Michael Johnson, Carl Lewis and Gail Devers.

In western states, rodeos with cowboys exhibiting bull and horse riding skills are popular sporting events. Recreational activities, such as hiking, walking, boating, hunting and fishing, are also popular.

In the swing

Tiger Woods's success has increased the popularity of golf in the USA. He has won most major golf championships at least once.

Entertainment capital

Surveys show that television is the biggest form of entertainment in the USA. Many children watch it for five or six hours every day. Viewers have a choice of dozens of channels, many of them devoted to one subject, such as shopping, films, religion or sport. The costs of making programmes are met by advertising revenue so American television programmes are frequently interrupted by commercial breaks. The USA produces a large number of high-quality television programmes, particularly comedy series and soap operas, which are popular not only in the USA, but all around the world. The USA is also the source of most of the world's best-known and most-watched films. Over 550 films are released in the USA

Pop power

Britney Spears is the biggest-selling teenage star. She has sold millions of records in the USA and throughout the rest of the world.

each year, mostly from the main centre of production in Hollywood, California, where studios have been making films since 1911. Successful films can make huge profits for the studios, so production companies are often prepared to invest tens of millions of US dollars in their most-favoured projects. This means they can employ the best directors, the most famous film stars and highly skilled technicians (cinematographers, lighting and sound engineers and make-up artists). They also use some of the most advanced special effects techniques. Every year a glamorous awards ceremony is held in Hollywood. The Academy Awards, or Oscars, celebrate the best films, directors and actors of the year.

The USA is also an innovator in music. Many of the trends in 20th-century music came from the USA. The blues played by African-Americans developed into jazz in the early 1900s, and later into rhythm and blues (R&B) and rock 'n' roll. Traditional American folk singing and country and western music have also had a major influence on modern pop music. Rock music is hugely popular in the USA and pop and rock stars can earn millions of US dollars. Rap and hip hop music developed in the black communities of US cities in the 1970s and 1980s, and is now part of mainstream US culture.

American composers have also produced many of the most popular stage musicals, such as *Kiss Me Kate* by Cole Porter, and *Oklahoma!* and *The Sound of Music* by Rodgers and Hammerstein. This worldwide influence also extends to the arts. After World War II, the USA produced many of the major trends in painting and sculpture, from the abstract expressionism of Jackson Pollock to the pop art of Andy Warhol. The USA has many excellent ballet companies and orchestras which stage classical music productions.

Movie mecca

Hollywood is home to the US film industry – and many film stars. Every year it hosts the Oscars award ceremony.

Industrial giant

The USA has rich resources – such as iron and other metals, coal and forests. It also has plenty of oil – but as the world's greatest consumer of oil, it still has to import much of what it needs, mainly from the Middle East. The USA is the world's leading producer of food and it provides for almost all of its own food needs. It exports large quantities of grain, grown mainly in the plains of the Midwest. Its industries manufacture world-famous brands of fizzy drinks, breakfast cereals, clothing, cars and aircraft. It also has

Wheat harvest

The Midwest states are nicknamed the 'bread basket' of the USA because of their huge fields of grains.

advanced scientific industries, producing new medicines and hi-tech hardware. NASA (National Aeronautics and Space Administration), the agency that was responsible for landing the first men on the moon in 1969, remains the world's leading organization for space exploration and satellite technology.

But the cost of labour is relatively high, and many goods bought in the USA are

Harnessing power

Mountain rivers such as this one in Utah have been dammed to drive hydroelectric power stations, which help meet some of the nation's vast energy needs.

Men on the moon

In 1969, US astronauts Neil Armstrong and Buzz Aldrin became the first humans to walk on the moon.

made abroad, in countries such as China, Malaysia and Bangladesh. In fact, the USA has a large trade deficit – the value of its imports is far greater than the value of its exports. The USA is in a stronger position with its financial services, such as insurance and its stock market, which is based in Wall Street in New York City.

About three-quarters of the US labour force no longer works in either industry or agriculture as it once did, but instead in service industries, such as finance, insurance, teaching, healthcare, tourism and real estate.

Rich and poor

The USA ranks among the top ten countries in the world in terms of national income per person, and the average American has more money to spend than the average citizen of just about any other country. The country has some 70 billionaires, far more than any other country. Yet many Americans are desperately poor. They live in the run-down suburbs of the cities, which are plagued by crime, violence, gang-warfare and drug abuse.

Low-income families with children, the disabled and the elderly can get some help from the government through the welfare

Homeless

Like many cities around the world, New York has many people who have no home and have to live on the streets, begging for food and making shelters in doorways.

system, but not a great deal. Essentially, in the USA, people are expected to fend for themselves. If they become ill, they are expected to pay for their treatment, which can be very expensive. Most people take out insurance policies to cover medical care, but the poorest often cannot afford to do so, and they have to rely on one of the basic government welfare systems, such as Medicare or Medicaid.

Crime and punishment

Many Americans are concerned about crime. In the USA over 15,000 people are murdered every year, and guns are used in at least two-thirds of these murders. There have also been several news reports of shootings in schools. Gun control – the effort to control the possession of guns and so reduce violent crime – is a major issue in the USA. Over half the families in the country have a gun in the household. Many Americans argue that guns are essential for self-protection in a world where violent crime is all too common. The Bill of Rights, added to the US Constitution in 1791 to protect the freedom of all American citizens, included the right to keep and bear arms – in other words, the right to possess guns and other weapons. But more and more people are calling for the number of guns on the streets to be reduced. One major cause of crime is drug abuse. This is the source of untold misery and death

Cop show

The uniform and cars of American police are familiar sights around the world because police often feature in movies and TV dramas. American police carry guns.

– not just from the drugs themselves, but the criminal activities that surround the trade in illegal drugs, which is worth billions of US dollars.

The USA has large and tough prisons, and more prisoners than any other country in the world – over 1.6 million. Many of the states have the death penalty, and convicted murderers can be executed. Prisoners condemned to die often live on the jail's 'death row' for many years while their lawyers lodge appeals in the courts in an attempt to overturn the death sentence.

There are some success stories in the country's fight against crime. The murder rate is declining. For many years New York City had a bad reputation for crime. But recently its police force applied a policy of 'zero tolerance' – they stopped anyone who was suspected of carrying out even a minor infringement, such as jumping over a park fence. The strategy seems to be working and New York City is now considered a comparatively safe city.

World power

The USA has been a force in world politics for over 100 years now. After World War II, it led the Western world in opposing the communist regimes of the Soviet Union and China. During the confrontation with the Soviet Union – called the 'Cold War' because it never turned into a real world war – both sides built up huge arsenals of nuclear weapons. By the time the Cold War ended with the collapse of the Soviet Union and its communist system of government in 1991, each side had enough nuclear weapons to destroy the world many times over. Today, the USA is the only superpower in the world and this has brought with it new responsibilities and concerns. The USA has become embroiled in conflicts which it views as a threat to world stability. In 1991, the USA led a coalition of countries to war against Iraq, which had invaded neighbouring Kuwait, and later in the same decade the USA was involved in peace-keeping efforts in Europe's troubled Balkan States.

The USA has a strong belief that its way of life and system of government are the best. This is based on protecting the freedom of its citizens and encouraging individuals to succeed. The nation has a powerful influence on the rest of the world through its films, television programmes, and its economic and military might. While many in the world see the US way of life as desirable, others resent

Stars and stripes

The US flag is called the 'Stars and Stripes'. It has 50 stars on it – one for each state. The red and white stripes represent the 13 original American colonies.

Powerful leader

As leader of the world's only superpower, the president of the United States is often called on to intervene in global conflicts. George W Bush is the country's 43rd president.

the influence of the USA. They see the imports of US movies, language and fast-food chains as a threat to their own countries' cultures and values.

Under threat

The political and military influence of the USA in the rest of the world has also earned it enemies. On 11 September 2001, an Islamic fundamentalist terrorist group called Al-Qaida hijacked planes and deliberately crashed them into the twin towers of the World Trade Center in New York City and the Pentagon in Washington DC. Thousands were killed in this terrorist attack and the US government launched a war against terrorism around the world, with the backing of many other countries. The first target was Afghanistan, where the terrorists behind the 11 September attack were believed to be hiding.

Many American people were shocked to find that there were some people who hated the USA so much that they were prepared to sacrifice themselves and kill so many civilians. As a result of the attack, many Americans became more aware of their country's status as the world's superpower, and the difficult responsibilities that this entails. However, the terrorist attack also gave the American people a renewed sense of patriotism and belief in the freedoms their nation enjoys.

CANADA

Canada is the second largest country in the world after Russia. Yet it only has a population of just over 30 million – or three people per km². Canada is mainly tundra (snowy, ice-bound wastes) in the far north with the dramatic Rocky Mountains to the west. The central plains contain vast prairies.

Almost all Canadians live in the southern part of the country, where temperatures are warmer – but even here the winters are long and cold, lasting from about November to April. Canada is well-prepared for the cold – the roads are quickly cleared by powerful snowploughs, the houses are well heated and insulated, people fit winter tyres to their cars, and they have cupboards full of warm, padded, winter clothes.

Canadians love winter sports such as skiing, tobogganing and ice-skating. There are major ski resorts, such as Whistler in the Coast Mountain Range and Mont Tremblant in Quebec. But the outdoor life is popular all year round, and in summer Canadians holiday among the lakes and woodlands, and go fishing and kayaking (canoeing).

Neighbourly differences

Canada has a long border with the USA. In fact, it is the world's longest land border, and most Canadians live within 200 km of it. This might suggest that Canadians are similar to Americans. It is true that they have much in common – they wear similar clothes, eat similar food, shop in large out-of-town malls, watch many of the same television programmes, play ice hockey, baseball and American-style football (but to Canadian rules).

Ice match
Ice hockey is very popular. Protective clothing is worn to break falls on the hard ice.

Children even go to school in the same kind of yellow buses. But the Canadians are quick to point out that they are by no means the same as Americans. Their attitude to life and the world at large is different. Over half the population has British or Irish origins, and Canada is an important member of the Commonwealth. The Queen, who is head of the Commonwealth, is also Canada's head of state and appears on their bank notes.

Canada has two official languages – English and French. The country has a sizeable French-speaking population, particularly in the eastern province of Quebec. French influence can be seen in architecture and food.

Shifting snow

The Canadians are used to coping with the long, cold winters. This man is using a snow mower to clear snow from his pathway.

French influence

The vast province of Quebec, stretching along the St Lawrence river and up to the Hudson Strait, is mainly French-speaking. The French were the earliest European settlers in Canada, founding the first community in 1605. They were absorbed into British Canada by conquest in 1763. The French Canadians, the Québecois, speak French with a distinctive accent, different from that spoken in France.

Each Canadian province is responsible for its own education system, and Quebec school

City life

The city of Quebec resembles a European city more than it does an American one. It is influenced by French architecture.

children are taught in French and learn English as a second language.

Representing nearly a quarter of Canada's total population, the people of Quebec still feel that they are a distinct group within Canada, and their relationship with English-speaking Canada is sometimes strained. Many Québecois would like to see Quebec become independent of the rest of Canada. When this idea was put to voters in 1995, a slim majority voted against it, arguing that Quebec needs the rest of Canada, and might not survive in isolation.

Native Americans

When the French first arrived in Canada in the early 17th century, the land was occupied by a number of native American groups, such as the Iroquois, the Algonquin and the Cree. Some still follow their traditional way of life in the remote lands of northern Canada, fishing and trapping animals for fur. Like other native Americans, however, many feel cheated of their ancestral lands. The Mohawks, for instance, are fiercely protective of their lands near Montreal.

For many years the Canadian government tried to assimilate native peoples into the rest of society, but in 1998, the government formally apologised to the native population for the way they had been mistreated. Native groups now receive funding to help them preserve their cultures and traditions.

The Inuit have lived in the far north for many thousands of years. In 1999, the Canadian government created a new territory called Nunavut for them, covering over two million km².

New ways

These Cree youths learn the culture and traditions of their people, but are also part of a cosmopolitan Canada – enjoying the best of both worlds.

Maple syrup and lumberjacks

The symbol of Canada is the red maple leaf, which appears on the flag. Maple trees create glorious colours in the autumn, turning the Canadian landscape not just red, but golden, yellow and orange too. In spring, a sweet, watery sap rises in the trunks of the maple trees. This can be tapped (collected) by cutting into the bark and attaching a container. The sap is then boiled to evaporate much of the water and to make a thick syrup. Canadians put maple syrup on pancakes and fried bacon at breakfast.

The forests are the source of another famous Canadian product – timber. Massive pine trees are cut down by lumberjacks (professional woodcutters), before being floated down the rivers to sawmills. Here they are turned into planks of timber, or ground into pulp to make paper. Canada also has valuable mineral resources such as copper, gold, iron and zinc, as well as oil and gas.

The Mounties

The Royal Canadian Mounted Police are nicknamed 'Mounties' and are Canada's national police force. Their distinctive red uniform is only worn for special parades.

Fishing is an important industry, and many of the towns and villages of eastern Canada, in Nova Scotia and the island of Newfoundland, developed as fishing ports. Recently, however, the Canadian fishing industry has been hit by the reduction in the numbers of cod in the north Atlantic and, in 1993, the Canadian government had to ban cod fishing to allow the stocks to recover.

Most Canadians live in the big cities. The capital of Canada is Ottawa, but the largest metropolitan area (city and suburbs) is Toronto, which has a population of over 4.3 million. Montreal, a city in the province of Quebec, comes second with a population of three million.

The third largest city, Vancouver (1.8 million), is on the west coast, with views over mountains, islands and sea inlets, and a milder climate than the rest of Canada. Whereas the rest of Canada tends to look towards the USA and Europe for trade, Vancouver forms part of the 'Pacific Rim', trading with China, Japan and South-east Asia.

Wood goods

Forestry is one of Canada's largest industries. It has vast forests, but environmentalists are concerned about the effects of the logging industry.

MEXICO

The Spanish-speaking country of Mexico borders the USA. It is a hot country with deserts in the north and arid mountains in the centre. In the far south there are sweltering tropical forests. Mexico is much poorer than its northern neighbour. The spending power of the average Mexican is about one-quarter that of the average American.

Ancient cultures

The great ancient civilizations of North America developed in Mexico, starting with the Olmecs in about 1200 BC, and leading to the Maya and the Aztecs. The impressive remains of their civilizations can be seen in many parts of Mexico. They include the pyramid temples of Teotihuacán and Chichén Itzá, and the collections of sculpture, pottery and jewellery at the National Museum of

The Maya
There are still Mayan villages in the Mexican rainforest. The Maya maintain many of their old customs and traditions and continue to speak Mayan languages.

Anthropology in the capital, Mexico City. But these civilizations collapsed with the conquest of Mexico in 1521 by the Spanish conquistador Hernán Cortés. The Spanish dominated the region until Mexico won its independence in 1836.

Many of the native Americans (or 'Indians' as they were called, because the first explorers mistakenly thought they had reached India), died from disease and maltreatment. Today, they make up a third of the population, while the rest are 'Mestizo' – a mixture of Spanish and native American. A quarter of all Mexicans live off the land, just as their ancient ancestors did, growing crops of beans, tomatoes, avocados and maize, which they use to make tortilla flat bread or crisp taco shells. Mexican food is often made spicy-hot with chilli peppers called jalapeños.

City life

Most Mexicans live in the towns and cities. Mexico City, the capital, is one of the world's largest cities, with a population of about 18 million. This huge number of people – many driving very old vehicles – gives Mexico City a serious pollution problem. Mexico has large reserves of oil, and it has thriving industries making steel, cars and electrical goods. It also attracts many tourists, with popular beach resorts, such as Acapulco and Cancún. But wages for the majority of Mexicans are low.

Day of the Dead

Many Mexican festivals are based on their Roman Catholic faith – but some have Aztec roots. For the Day of the Dead fiesta, families go to cemeteries to light candles and offer gifts to the dead, who are thought to return to visit the living for the day. To welcome them, shops and homes are decorated with models of skeletons, made of papier-mâché or dough.

Tortillas

Tortillas are thin round patties of maize- or wheat-flour dough cooked on griddles. They are often served along with a meal, or fried to make tacos.

Coastal resort

Tourists flock to the Pacific coast resort of Acapulco with its white sand beaches, high-rise hotels and hectic nightlife. Tourism is the main industry of the area.

THE CARIBBEAN

Hundreds of islands lie scattered across the Caribbean Sea. They are famous for their sandy beaches, warm, turquoise-blue seas and easy-going lifestyle. Thirteen of these are independent countries. The largest is Cuba, which is bigger than all the other islands put together. The smallest is St Kitts and Nevis, at just 262 km².

Caribs and slaves

The Caribbean Sea is named after the Carib Indians who lived on many of the islands before the arrival of Christopher Columbus (the first European explorer) in 1492. There is still a small population of Caribs on the islands of Dominica and St Vincent, but most of the Carib Indians were wiped out by illness and maltreatment, not long after the islands were taken over and settled by European countries. Spanish, British, French and Dutch colonizers wanted to use the islands to grow valuable crops of sugar cane. With few Carib Indians left, they needed labour to work in the plantations, so they imported slaves from western Africa. The vast majority of the population in the Caribbean islands today are the descendants of these slaves.

Each island has its own story to tell, and its own mix of peoples. In Cuba, for instance, many of the people are descended from Spanish settlers. Some of the people living in the islands of St Vincent and the Grenadines are descendants of Cornish fishermen, who settled in the region over 200 years ago.

When slavery was abolished in the 19th century, plantation owners found a new source of cheap labour in Asia, and brought in workers from India and China. Today, 40 per cent of the population of Trinidad and Tobago are Asian.

Cuban cigars

Tobacco plants are grown in Cuba. The leaves are picked, dried and rolled to make their world-famous cigars.

Making a living

One of the legacies of slavery is that the islands are heavily populated. They have a large number of mouths to feed, and most islands have few resources – Haiti is the poorest country of all the Americas.

Sugar cane is no longer the source of great riches. Desperate to seek more prosperous lives, many people from the Caribbean islands have left their homes and emigrated abroad. There are now large Haitian

communities in the USA and Canada. Many thousands of people from the West Indies (as the former British islands are known) went to live in Britain.

The islands have had to find other means to earn an income. Some have natural resources: Trinidad has a wealth of oil; Jamaica has bauxite (aluminium ore); and Cuba has oil, as well as nickel, copper and chrome. Other islands grow crops for export. St Lucia grows bananas; St Vincent is the world's largest producer of arrowroot, a starch used as a food thickener, and to make medicines and paper; Jamaica grows a high-quality coffee in its Blue Mountains; and Grenada produces spices, such as cloves and nutmeg. Many islands produce rum from sugar cane.

Another way of earning income is through tourism. The Caribbean islands have all-year warmth, perfect beaches, and beautiful coral reefs for divers.

Holiday haven

Luxury resorts have been built on some Caribbean islands, such as Barbados. Tourists come from all over the world.

Caribbean rhythms

In many parts of the Caribbean, tourism brings little direct benefit to the people. Living on extremely low incomes, they survive by growing vegetables and fruit, such as yams, mangoes and papayas, raising a few pigs and chickens, and fishing from small boats. They live in wooden houses, with corrugated iron roofs. These are vulnerable to the devastating hurricanes that sweep through the region, demolishing all in their path. Living in such conditions is hard, but the people of the

Colourful carnival

Most Caribbean countries hold annual carnivals where participants wear colourful costumes and dance through the street to musical rhythms.

Caribbean are famous for enjoying themselves. The distinctive forms of Caribbean music reflect the history of the islands – African rhythms, Spanish guitar and English folk-singing. They have produced calypso, salsa, rumba and soca, and in Trinidad, the sounds of steel bands, produced by hitting hammered oil drums. Most famous of all, perhaps, is reggae, the music of Jamaica.

Caribbeans feel that they still live in the shadow of their old European colonial rulers, and the power of the USA to the north.

Cuba has taken a unique path of defiant independence. In 1959, the corrupt regime of President Fulgencio Batista was overthrown by a revolution led by a young lawyer, Fidel Castro. When the USA refused to help Castro, he looked to the Soviet Union for assistance, and turned his country into a communist state. Despite Soviet help, there was little money to go around, food was rationed, and most Cubans lived in crumbling houses, using old American cars dating from the 1950s. In 1991, the Soviet Union collapsed, and soon after Russia withdrew its support. Facing a new crisis, Castro rapidly developed a new tourist industry to attract foreign income.

Despite the poverty, Cubans enjoy one of the best health services of the region, the old are cared for, and there is little crime. The Cubans are also proud that they have created an alternative way of life, which is sociable and caring, though poor. But there are doubts that it will survive when Castro is no longer there to enforce his policies.

Independent means

Reggae is closely associated with the Rastafarian movement, a religion that developed among the young people of Jamaica, focusing on their African heritage. This represented one way in which the people of the Caribbean have tried to express their unique history and identity, and desire for independence. Many

Cuban rhythms

Cuban music has its origins with the African slaves who were brought to the island. Stringed instruments such as the guitar and double bass are very popular.

CENTRAL AMERICA

A chain of seven small countries links Mexico and North America to South America. The tapering ribbon of land called Central America separates the Atlantic Ocean from the Pacific Ocean by just 50 km of low-lying swampland at its narrowest point in Panama. Elsewhere, the landscape rises from coasts to forests and volcanic peaks, and mountains dotted with lakes.

Young helpers

Young Mayan girls have to help their mothers take care of their younger brothers and sisters. Sometimes this means missing out on going to school.

Tribal cultures

In ancient times large areas of these countries were inhabited by people ruled by, or connected to, the Maya. The ruins of several great Mayan temple-cities are found in the north of the region, such as Tikal in Guatemala and Copán in Honduras. There may be others as yet undiscovered, hidden by the dense thickets of trees and undergrowth that grow rapidly in the warmth, heavy rains and rich, tropical soil of this region.

These days, many of the native American descendants work the same soil, growing the same plants, such as maize, sweet potatoes and cocoa. They also wear clothes that reflect their distinctive heritage. The women, for instance, wear brightly coloured woven jackets, shawls and headscarves. In Guatemala, native American women wear blouses with emblems embroidered on them, showing the Mayan clan to which they belong. Nearly half the population of Guatemala is native American, and most of the remaining half are 'Ladinos' (a mix of Spanish and native American).

Isolation has helped to protect the traditional ways of some native Americans, such as the Cuna people who live on the San Blas Islands, off the Caribbean coast of Panama. The women wear nose rings, heavy necklaces of beads or silver coins, and embroidered armbands. They use berry juice to mark their faces with lines. On the islands, the Cuna live in palm-walled huts and sleep in hammocks. They fish from small boats and come to the mainland forests to grow food in clearings.

Lakeside crops

Guatemala is the Mayan heartland of Central America. Farmers grow crops of maize and beans, squash and tomatoes on the banks of Lake Atitlán.

European influence

The Spanish conquered Central America in the 16th century. This is why the official language of most of the countries is Spanish, although other native American languages are spoken, many of them related to Mayan. One exception is Belize, where the official language is English, because up until 1981, Belize was ruled by the British. About 20 per cent of the population of Belize are native American, while almost a third are African-American, the descendants of slaves.

Most of the people of Central America are Roman Catholics, and attend services at churches built by the Spanish. Many are elaborate, with interiors richly encrusted with gold and statues of the saints. But local people also bring their own influence to Roman Catholicism, mixing it with ancient traditional beliefs, lighting candles and incense for their own gods, and following their ancient rituals.

Living off the land

The main source of income for most of these countries is agriculture. Honduras, for instance, grows vast quantities of bananas and pineapples on huge plantations. Most of the produce is exported, particularly to the USA. Coffee is another big export crop. Costa Rica and Nicaragua are especially famous for their coffee. A speciality of El Salvador is sweet-smelling balsam gum, a tree-resin used in perfumes and ointments. Cattle are raised on ranches in the rich grasslands of Costa Rica and Panama, herded by gauchos (cowboys).

The economy of Panama is based on its famous canal. This vital shipping link was carved through the jungle to provide a passage between the Pacific and the Atlantic. Before it was completed in 1914, large ships travelling between the east coast of the USA and the west coast had to go all the way around the southern tip of South America. The USA ran the Panama Canal until 2000. But it is now owned and operated by Panama, and the country earns millions of US dollars from the fees paid by ships passing through it.

Panama Canal

The Panama Canal is an incredible feat of engineering. It spans 80 km from the Pacific to the Atlantic Oceans and was completed in 1914.

Panama hats

The famous, delicately woven Panama hats originated in Ecuador, but were worn as protective hats by many of the workers on the Panama Canal.

Instability and opportunity

Central America has suffered from two sources of instability – nature and politics. The hills and mountains are frequently shaken by earthquakes. Added to this, hurricanes frequently sweep through the region from the Caribbean. Belize moved its capital to Belmopan after a hurricane demolished the old capital, Belize City, in 1961. In 1998, Hurricane Mitch ripped through Honduras, Nicaragua and Guatemala. The high winds and huge torrents of water destroyed much of Managua, the capital of Nicaragua, and tore up houses, roads and plantations. Some 10,000 people were killed.

Such natural disasters add to the severe economic problems in these countries. The annual income across the region is about one-tenth that of the USA. In the farmlands in the central highlands of El Salvador, for example, families live in simple thatched homes made of wattle (tree branches plastered with mud). On the flat, coastal lands of eastern Nicaragua, villagers live in wooden shacks built on stilts, so that they can escape the heavy rains. They use ox-carts, which are better suited to the poor, muddy roads than cars or lorries.

Many people come to the cities, hoping to find work, but end up living in poor shanty towns.

Poverty has played its part in the violent politics of this region. In the past, corrupt regimes in El Salvador, Nicaragua and Guatemala, attempting to protect the advantages of the wealthy few, have faced armed rebellion from communist groups. Costa Rica has escaped such troubles, and does not have an army at all, having abolished it over 50 years ago.

Tourism is one way in which Central American countries can boost their incomes. Costa Rica has chosen to take advantage of its magnificent tropical forests, which are home to rare species such as sloths, jaguars and poison-arrow frogs. It has declared large parts of the country to be nature reserves.

Deadly storm

Hurricane Mitch brought devastation to Central America in 1998. Relief workers cleared debris and brought food and clean water to the people affected.

Rural life

Many people in the region live in villages and have few goods and very little money. They make their living growing such crops as wheat.

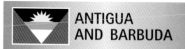

ANTIGUA AND BARBUDA

Capital
St John's, on Antigua
Area
442 km²
Population
67,000
Population density
152 per km²
Life expectancy
74 (m); 74 (f)
Religion
Christianity
Languages
English, English patois
Adult literacy rate
90 per cent
Currency
East Caribbean dollar

BAHAMAS

Capital
Nassau, on New Providence
Area
13,939 km²
Population
301,000
Population density
22 per km²
Life expectancy
68 (m); 75 (f)
Religion
Christianity
Language
English
Adult literacy rate
98 per cent
Currency
Bahamian dollar

BARBADOS

Capital
Bridgetown
Area
431 km²
Population
267,000
Population density
617 per km²
Life expectancy
70 (m); 76 (f)
Religion
Christianity
Language
English
Adult literacy rate
97 per cent
Currency
Barbados dollar

Island paradise

The Caribbean island of Barbados attracts thousands of tourists every year with its tropical climate, palm trees and sandy beaches.

BELIZE

Capital
Belmopan
Area
22,965 km²
Population
235,000
Population density
10 per km²
Life expectancy
70 (m); 74 (f)
Religion
Christianity
Languages
English, Spanish, Creole,
Gariguna, Maya, Ketchi,
German
Adult literacy rate
90 per cent
Currency
Belize dollar

 **CANADA**

Capital
Ottawa
Area
9,958,319 km²
Population
30,491,000
Population density
3 per km²
Life expectancy
74 (m); 81 (f)
Religion
Christianity
Languages
English, French and
local languages
Adult literacy rate
99 per cent
Currency
Canadian dollar

 COSTA RICA

Capital
San José
Area
51,100 km²
Population
3,589,000
Population density
69 per km²
Life expectancy
73 (m); 78 (f)
Religion
Christianity
Languages
Spanish, patois
Adult literacy rate
95 per cent
Currency
Costa Rican colón

 **CUBA**

Capital
Havana
Area
110,860 km²
Population
11,160,000
Population density
100 per km²
Life expectancy
74 (m); 77 (f)
Religion
Christianity
Language
Spanish
Adult literacy rate
96 per cent
Currency
Cuban peso

 DOMINICA

Capital
Roseau
Area
750 km²
Population
71,000
Population density
107 per km²
Life expectancy
72 (m); 72 (f)
Religion
Christianity
Languages
English, French, patois
Adult literacy rate
94 per cent
Currency
East Caribbean dollar

 DOMINICAN REPUBLIC

Capital
Santo Domingo
Area
48,422 km²
Population
8,348,000
Population density
167 per km²
Life expectancy
68 (m); 72 (f)
Religion
Christianity
Language
Spanish
Adult literacy rate
82 per cent
Currency
Dominican Republic peso

EL SALVADOR

Capital
San Salvador
Area
21,041 km²
Population
6,154,000
Population density
287 per km²
Life expectancy
51 (m); 64 (f)
Religion
Christianity
Languages
Spanish and local languages
Adult literacy rate
71 per cent
Currency
US dollar and Salvadorean colón

 GRENADA

Capital
St George's
Area
344 km²
Population
93,000
Population density
270 per km²
Life expectancy
71 (m); 71 (f)
Religion
Christianity
Languages
English, French, patois
Adult literacy rate
90 per cent
Currency
East Caribbean dollar

 GUATEMALA

Capital
Guatemala City
Area
108,889 km²
Population
11,088,000
Population density
99 per km²
Life expectancy
62 (m); 67 (f)
Religion
Christianity
Languages
Spanish and local languages
Adult literacy rate
56 per cent
Currency
quetzal

HAITI

Capital
Port-au-Prince
Area
27,750 km²
Population
7,803,000
Population density
276 per km²
Life expectancy
52 (m); 56 (f)
Religions
Christianity, Voodoo (a blend of Christianity and traditional African beliefs)
Languages
French, Creole
Adult literacy rate
45 per cent
Currency
gourde

HONDURAS

Capital
Tegucigalpa
Area
112,088 km²
Population
6,385,000
Population density
55 per km²
Life expectancy
65 (m); 70 (f)
Religion
Christianity
Languages
Spanish, English and local languages
Adult literacy rate
73 per cent
Currency
lempira

 **JAMAICA**

Capital
Kingston
Area
10,991 km²
Population
2,590,000
Population density
231 per km²
Life expectancy
71 (m); 76 (f)
Religion
Christianity
Languages
English, patois
Adult literacy rate
85 per cent
Currency
Jamaican dollar

MEXICO

Capital
Mexico City
Area
1,958,201 km²
Population
97,361,711
Population density
48 per km²
Life expectancy
68 (m); 74 (f)
Religion
Christianity
Languages
Spanish and local languages
Adult literacy rate
90 per cent
Currency
Mexican peso

 NICARAGUA

Capital
Managua
Area
120,254 km²
Population
4,936,000
Population density
40 per km²
Life expectancy
63 (m); 69 (f)
Religion
Christianity
Languages
Spanish, English and local
languages
Adult literacy rate
66 per cent
Currency
gold córdoba

 **PANAMA**

Capital
Panama City
Area
75,517 km²
Population
2,809,000
Population density
37 per km²
Life expectancy
71 (m); 76 (f)
Religion
Christianity
Languages
Spanish and local languages
Adult literacy rate
91 per cent
Currency
US dollar and balboa

 **ST KITTS AND NEVIS**

Capital
Basseterre, on St Kitts
Area
261 km²
Population
41,000
Population density
157 per km²
Life expectancy
67 (m); 70 (f)
Religion
Christianity
Language
English
Adult literacy rate
97 per cent
Currency
East Caribbean dollar

 ST LUCIA

Capital
Castries
Area
616 km²
Population
146,000
Population density
237 per km²
Life expectancy
69 (m); 75 (f)
Religion
Christianity
Languages
English, French, patois
Adult literacy rate
81 per cent
Currency
East Caribbean dollar

 ST VINCENT AND THE GRENADINES

Capital
Kingstown, on St Vincent
Area
389 km²
Population
112,000
Population density
288 per km²
Life expectancy
72 (m); 72 (f)
Religion
Christianity
Languages
English, French
Adult literacy rate
82 per cent
Currency
East Caribbean dollar

TRINIDAD AND TOBAGO

Capital
Port of Spain, on Trinidad
Area
5,128 km²
Population
1,289,000
Population density
250 per km²
Life expectancy
72 (m); 72 (f)
Religions
Christianity, Hinduism
Languages
English, French, Spanish, Hindi, Chinese
Adult literacy rate
98 per cent
Currency
Trinidad and Tobago dollar

UNITED STATES OF AMERICA

Capital
Washington DC
Area
9,809,155 km²
Population
281,422,000
Population density
28 per km²
Life expectancy
72 (m); 79 (f)
Religions
Christianity, Judaism, Islam
Languages
English, Spanish and many native languages
Adult literacy rate
99 per cent
Currency
US dollar

Stars and stripes

The USA has a strong sense of national identity, and the Stars and Stripes flag is proudly displayed on national holidays.

South America

Brazil

SOUTH AMERICA

Caribbean
Sea

■ Caracas

Apure *Orinoco*

Gulf of Panama

Llanos VENEZUELA
Guiana GUYANA
Highlands ■ Georgetown
Paramaribo ■
■ Bogotá *Guaviare* SURINAM Cayenne ■
French
Guiana

ATLANTIC
OCEAN

COLOMBIA

Caquetá *Rio Negro*

Quito ■ *Japurá* A M A Z O N
ECUADOR *Putumayo* *Amazon* Marajó
Amazon

*Gulf of
Guayaquil* *Marañón*
Ucayali B A S I N *Madeira* *Tapajós* *Iriri*
Iurua *Selvas* *Purus* *Teles Pires* *Xingu*
B R A Z I L

PERU *Madre de Dios* *São Francisco*
Lima ■ *Beni* *Guaporé* *Juruena* *Araguaia* *Tocantins* *Sobradinho
Reservoir*

BOLIVIA *Mato Grosso
Plateau*
*Lake
Titicaca*
■ La Paz Brasília ■ *Brazilian
Highlands*
Altiplano Sucre ■

PACIFIC
OCEAN *Atacama Desert* *Gran Chaco* PARAGUAY
Pilcomayo
Paraguay
Asunción ■
Salado *Paraná*
Uruguay

*Mar
Chiquita* *Patos
Lagoon*
URUGUAY
*Mirim
Lake*
Santiago ■ Aconcagua
6960m Montevideo ■
*Juan
Fernández Is.* Buenos Aires ■
ARGENTINA *Rio de la Plata*
Pampas
Colorado

Río Negro

*San Matías
Gulf*

Chiloé I.

Los Chonos
Archipelago ATLANTIC
San Jorge OCEAN
Gulf

Falkland Islands
(Islas Malvinas)
(UK)
Wellington I.
West ■ Stanley
*Bahía
Grande* Falkland East Falkland
Reina Adelaida
Archipelago *Strait of Magellan*

Tierra
Del Fuego
South Georgia
Cape Horn (UK)

	Mountain
	Desert
	Tundra
	Cropland
	Wetland
	Needleleaf forest
	Tropical rainforest
	Temperate grassland
	Ice

N

0   500   1000 km
0   250   500 miles

Amazon

*The Amazon
Basin contains
the largest area
of tropical
forest in the
world, and more
plant and animal
species than any
other habitat.*

SOUTH AMERICA

South America is a continent of immense richness and variety. In the far north, Venezuela and Colombia have palm-fringed coasts on the warm Caribbean Sea. In the far south, Chile and Argentina reach down to the bitterly cold island of Tierra del Fuego, just 1,000 km from Antarctica. Ushuaia, the capital of Argentine-controlled Tierra del Fuego, is the world's most southerly town.

The Andes forms a mighty chain of soaring mountains that runs up the western side of the continent. Chile, a long thin ribbon of land, is practically all mountain and coastline. Bolivia, Peru, Ecuador and Colombia all have extensive mountain regions. La Paz in Bolivia is the world's highest capital city, at 3,660 m above sea level – so high that the air is thin, from lack of oxygen, and visitors become quite breathless until their bodies get used to the altitude. The central-west coast has stretches of hot and extremely dry desert. To the east of the Andes is the Amazon Basin, a vast region of damp, steamy tropical forest.

Life in Bolivia

A Bolivian woman carries a child on her back, wrapped snugly against the cold of the Andes Mountains.

Remnants of European rule

Like Central America, most of the South American countries are Spanish-speaking. The exception is Brazil, where the national language is Portuguese. In the past, these countries were ruled as colonies by Spain and Portugal. Three small countries on the north-east coast have a slightly different history. English is spoken in Guyana, which used to be ruled by the British, and cricket is still the national sport there. Surinam was governed by the Netherlands, and the official language is Dutch. Next to Surinam is French Guiana, which is still ruled by France.

Settlers from these European countries came to live in South America, and between the 16th and 19th centuries, they transported hundreds of thousands of slaves from Africa to work in the plantations. The slaves were later joined by plantation workers from India, China and Indonesia, by traders from Syria and Lebanon, and farmers and industrialists from Italy, Germany and Scandinavia. This created the great mix of ethnic groups that is so characteristic of South America.

Church parade

Children in a Colombian town join a candlelit procession in Holy Week, the week before Easter.

Llama farmers

Llamas are native to South America. They are raised in herds for their meat and their wool, which is used to make warm clothes.

Native Americans

Before the Europeans came in the early 16th century, South America was occupied by different groups of native South Americans, who, like the native Central Americans, later became known incorrectly as 'Indians'. Much of the Andes was ruled as a powerful empire under the Inca of Peru – the largest native group.

These native Americans were largely farmers, who built elaborate terraces on the hillsides to grow crops of potatoes and maize, and raised llamas to carry their goods along the network of high mountain paths. Other native peoples lived lives that similarly reflected their surroundings, fishing off the coasts, or growing crops in the valleys of rivers. The forest peoples of the Amazon Basin built villages in clearings, and lived by gathering plants and fruit, and hunting in the forest.

Floating high

This Peruvian child is in a reed boat on Lake Titicaca, which lies 3,810 m above sea level in the Andes Mountains.

Poncho protection

To keep warm in the mountains, the native Americans in Ecuador wear ponchos (a large piece of cloth with a hole for the head).

There are still a large number of native Americans in South America. Some live by hunting, fishing and growing root crops in the remote tropical forests of the Amazon Basin. High in the Andes of Ecuador, Otavaleño Indians live in small, white-washed villages built of adobe mud-brick. They tend sheep and grow maize and potatoes, much as their ancestors did, but today their brightly coloured woven cloth is sold in the tourist market of Otavalo. These days, the majority of people in South America are 'Mestizos' (mixed Spanish and native American descent).

Bolivian piper

Bolivian music is famous for its soaring, graceful sound. It is played on instruments such as the queña (panpipes made from bamboo) and the charango (a guitar made from the shell of an armadillo).

Most South American countries are Spanish-speaking and most highly paid, professional jobs are done by people of Spanish descent living in the towns and cities.

Many native Americans live in the countryside, and some people of European origin still discriminate against them. When Alejandro Toledo, a candidate of native American ancestry, was elected president of Peru in 2001, it was considered remarkable, even though half the population is native American.

Coffee and chocolate

Large areas of South America are used for farming. In the warmer regions, coffee, cocoa and sugar cane are grown on huge plantations. Grapes to make wine are grown in the cooler regions of Chile and Argentina.

Cattle are raised in the llanos (hot plains) of southern Venezuela, but the most famous cattle ranches are in the open pampas grasslands of Argentina and Uruguay. Here, the herds are looked after by skilled gauchos (cowboys), who ride on horseback wearing broad-rimmed hats, baggy trousers and high boots.

Gauchos eat asado – beef barbecued on a spit by an open fire. They drink a type of tea called 'yerba maté'.

Sun beans

After harvesting, coffee beans are spread on concrete floors or tables to dry in the sun. They are turned regularly. for 7 to 15 days.

Horse skills

Horse-riding skills are highly valued in South America and many children learn to ride at a young age. This boy is showing his skills at a festival in Chile.

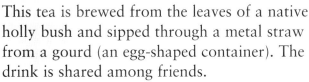

This tea is brewed from the leaves of a native holly bush and sipped through a metal straw from a gourd (an egg-shaped container). The drink is shared among friends.

Food differs from country to country, but a typical meal across the region consists of a piece of fried beef or chicken, eaten with rice or boiled potatoes and salad, and served with fried plantains, a banana-like vegetable. Tasty snacks include charcoal-grilled maize and empanadas (spicy, savoury pastries).

It is hard to make a living by farming in many regions in South America. This is why some farmers, especially in Colombia, have turned to growing crops that are used to make illegal drugs, such as cocaine and marijuana. The drug trade, run by armed criminal gangs, causes terror and instability in the region. Exported largely to the USA, the drug crops earn the farmers vast sums of money. South American governments struggle to persuade the farmers to grow alternative crops. The farmers are worried they will not earn enough to feed their families.

Shanty towns

The majority of South Americans live in towns and cities. Most of these were founded by European settlers from the 16th century onwards, but their old historic centres, with their grand palaces and their richly decorated Roman Catholic churches, are now surrounded by modern high-rise buildings and streets busy with traffic.

Poor families come to the cities from the countryside in the hope of finding work. But work is not always easy to find, and many of them end up living in shacks in the shanty towns on the outskirts of the cities, without running water, proper drainage or proper electricity supplies. Furthermore, the shanty towns are often built on poor, steep land and can be washed away in heavy storms.

Many of the poorest children from the shanty towns cannot afford to go to school as they have to earn money for food – although education is usually free up to the age of 14. Some do not have homes, but sleep on the streets, sheltering in cardboard boxes. These 'street children' may scratch a living by doing odd jobs, begging or stealing.

Poverty is a problem that faces most countries in South America. Many are rich in resources – Venezuela, Ecuador and Argentina have oil, Brazil has gold and iron ore, Chile has copper, Colombia has coal and emeralds, Bolivia has tin and natural gas, and Guyana and Brazil have bauxite (aluminium ore).

They also have plenty of fertile land. But their economies are not strong enough to

Football fans

South American national football teams often compete against teams from around the world in international contests. Millions of fans watch the matches on television.

Fetching water

Most shanty towns do not have clean water supplies and people have to buy containers of it. Cholera, a disease caused by dirty water, is a problem in many South American countries.

have been replaced by democratic governments, but economic difficulties have continued to cause instability. In early 2002, Argentina's huge debts to foreign banks made the country virtually bankrupt.

Culture and sport

The colourful, varied and complex world of South America has been captured by some of its best-known writers, such as Jorge Luis Borges of Argentina, and Gabriel García Márquez of Colombia. It is also reflected in the music, from the rhythmic folk-songs played with guitars, accordions, tambourines and the Andean panpipes, to the passionate up-tempo music of the tango, the fiery dance of Argentina.

The most popular sport in South America is football. Children practise their football skills from an early age, hoping one day to become a professional footballer. The great star of Argentinian football of the 1980s, Diego Maradona, was brought up in a shanty town in the capital, Buenos Aires. His foot-juggling tricks helped him become a professional footballer at the age of just 15.

In Bogotá, the capital of Colombia, street children play a more dangerous game, clinging on to the bumpers of moving buses and 'surfing' on flattened wooden fruit crates.

guarantee long-term wealth for their people. As a result, they have suffered from unstable governments. Most countries have been taken over by military dictators in the past, and some of these have been particularly cruel. When Argentina was under military rule in the 1970s, at least 30,000 young people 'disappeared'. In a ruthless effort to stamp out left-wing terrorism, they were murdered by government agents, or died in prison. Since the 1980s, all the military dictators

Gold mining

Brazil, Peru and Venezuela are among the South American countries with gold supplies. Thousands of miners dig the ground searching for gold deposits.

BRAZIL

Brazil is by far the largest country in South America. Its main language is Portuguese, not Spanish – Brazil was a Portuguese colony for over three hundred years, until 1822. The north of the country is home to the densely forested Amazon Basin. The city of Rio de Janeiro lies on the coast and is famous for its colourful carnivals.

All the world

When Brazil became a Portuguese colony in 1500, it was already populated by about two million native Americans. Many of them were killed in war or by disease, or pushed back into the forests. The Portuguese established plantations to grow sugar cane, coffee, cocoa and cotton, and they brought about four million west African slaves to the country to work on these plantations.

The European settlers stayed mainly around the coasts, where they were joined by people from all over the world. These early settlers have created a country with a huge mix of peoples and cultures. The greatest showpiece of Brazil's vibrant energy is its famous carnival week in Rio de Janeiro. Performers dressed in amazing, colourful costumes parade through the streets dancing to the samba – a heady blend of European music and African rhythms.

Natural wealth

Brazil has rich resources. The mines produce gold, iron ore and bauxite (aluminium ore). There is also oil and natural gas. Brazil is South America's leading industrial nation, and its factories produce cars, aeroplanes, textiles and processed foods. It is also the world's largest producer of sugar and coffee.

Rio de Janeiro

Rio de Janeiro lies among rainforest-clad cliffs on the Atlantic coast. Its beautiful scenery and beaches make it a popular tourist destination.

Colourful carnival

Work on the lavish carnival costumes begins months before the event. The date varies from year to year but it is usually held during the peak of summer.

The Amazon river is the most important geographical feature of Brazil. It is the world's second longest river after the Nile, and has a network of rivers leading off it, forming the Amazon Basin. Much of the Amazon Basin is swampland and forest – it is the world's largest tropical rainforest. Roads have been built through the forest to open up the region for development. Loggers cut down the trees for timber, and international companies mine for gold and bauxite. Farmers use the cleared land to grow crops and raise cattle. As a result, large areas of forest have been destroyed.

The Amazon rainforest is home to native Americans who follow patterns of life that have changed very little for thousands of years. They hunt with poison arrows, live in round thatched homes, and use forest plants as medicine. But many of the forest's peoples have seen their lives change dramatically as industries and new settlers invade their land.

The Brazilian government has to make difficult choices. On the one hand, it wants to preserve the forest and the people who live there. On the other, it wants its people to prosper, by exploiting the country's resources. As a symbol of its desire to modernize, in 1961 Brazil created an entirely new capital, called Brasília, closer to the centre of the country than the old capital Rio de Janeiro.

ARGENTINA

Capital
Buenos Aires
Area
2,766,889 km²
Population
36,578,000
Population density
13 per km²
Life expectancy
68 (m); 73 (f)
Religion
Christianity
Languages
Spanish, many other European languages and local languages
Adult literacy rate
96 per cent
Currency
Argentine peso

BOLIVIA

Capital
La Paz (administrative);
Sucre (judicial)
Area
1,098,581 km²
Population
8,137,000
Population density
7 per km²
Life expectancy
59 (m); 63 (f)
Religion
Christianity
Languages
Spanish, Quechua, Aymara
Adult literacy rate
83 per cent
Currency
Boliviano

BRAZIL

Capital
Brasília
Area
8,511,996 km²
Population
165,371,000
Population density
19 per km²
Life expectancy
64 (m); 70 (f)
Religion
Christianity
Languages
Portuguese and local languages
Adult literacy rate
85 per cent
Currency
real

CHILE

Capital
Santiago
Area
756,626 km²
Population
15,018,000
Population density
20 per km²
Life expectancy
72 (m); 77 (f)
Religion
Christianity
Languages
Spanish, Araucanian
Adult literacy rate
95 per cent
Currency
Chilean peso

COLOMBIA

Capital
Bogotá
Area
1,141,748 km²
Population
41,589,000
Population density
36 per km²
Life expectancy
66 (m); 72 (f)
Religion
Christianity
Language
Spanish
Adult literacy rate
91 per cent
Currency
Colombian peso

ECUADOR

Capital
Quito
Area
272,045 km²
Population
12,411,000
Population density
45 per km²
Life expectancy
67 (m); 72 (f)
Religion
Christianity
Languages
Spanish, Quechua and local languages
Adult literacy rate
90 per cent
Currency
US dollar

Learning to hunt

These children live in the Amazon Basin in Brazil. They are learning how to use a bow and arrow so they can hunt for food.

GUYANA

Capital
Georgetown
Area
214,969 km²
Population
855,000
Population density
4 per km²
Life expectancy
62 (m); 68 (f)
Religions
Christianity, Hinduism, Islam
Languages
English, Hindi, Urdu and local dialects
Adult literacy rate
98 per cent
Currency
Guyanese dollar

 PARAGUAY

Capital
Asunción
Area
406,752 km²
Population
5,356,000
Population density
13 per km²
Life expectancy
66 (m); 70 (f)
Religion
Christianity
Languages
Spanish, Guarani
Adult literacy rate
92 per cent
Currency
guarani

 PERU

Capital
Lima
Area
1,285,216 km²
Population
25,232,000
Population density
19 per km²
Life expectancy
66 (m); 70 (f)
Religion
Christianity
Languages
Spanish, Quechua, Aymara
Adult literacy rate
89 per cent
Currency
new sol

 SURINAM

Capital
Paramaribo
Area
163,265 km²
Population
415,000
Population density
3 per km²
Life expectancy
64 (m); 71 (f)
Religions
Christianity, Hinduism, Islam
Languages
Dutch, Hindi, Javanese, Sranang Tongo, Chinese, English
Adult literacy rate
93 per cent
Currency
Surinam guilder

 URUGUAY

Capital
Montevideo
Area
176,215 km²
Population
3,313,000
Population density
19 per km²
Life expectancy
68 (m); 74 (f)
Religion
Christianity
Languages
Spanish, Portuguese
Adult literacy rate
97 per cent
Currency
Uruguayan peso

VENEZUELA

Capital
Caracas
Area
912,050 km²
Population
23,706,000
Population density
25 per km²
Life expectancy
69 (m); 75 (f)
Religion
Christianity
Languages
Spanish and local languages
Adult literacy rate
91 per cent
Currency
bolívar

Northern Africa

Eastern Africa

Western Africa

Central Africa

Southern Africa

AFRICA

Early civilization

The pyramids in Egypt were built thousands of years ago as tombs for the pharaohs, rulers of an ancient civilization.

Algiers
Tunis
TUNISIA
Rabat
MOROCCO
Atlas Mountains
Mediterranean Sea
Tripoli
Gulf of Sirte
Cairo
ALGERIA
LIBYA
Libyan Desert
EGYPT
Red Sea
Laâyoune
WESTERN SAHARA
S A H A R A
Erg Chech
Tassili-n-Ajjer
Ahaggar
Ténéré
Tibesti
Lake Nasser
Nubian Desert
MAURITANIA
Nouakchott
MALI
Aïr
NIGER
Niger
Khartoum
ERITREA
Asmara
SENEGAL
Dakar
Senegal
S A H E L
CHAD
SUDAN
Blue Nile
Atbara
Gulf of Aden
DJIBOUTI
Djibouti
GAMBIA
Banjul
Bamako
BURKINA FASO
Niamey
Lake Chad
N'djamena
Chari
White Nile
Ethiopian Highlands
Addis Ababa
GUINEA BISSAU
Bissau
GUINEA
Ouagdougou
Niger
Bahr el Ghazal
ETHIOPIA
Horn of Africa
Conakry
SIERRA LEONE
Freetown
COTE D'IVOIRE
L. Volta
GHANA
TOGO
BENIN
Abuja
Benue
NIGERIA
CENTRAL AFRICAN REPUBLIC
Uele
SOMALIA
Mogadishu
Monrovia
LIBERIA
Yamoussoukro
Accra
Lomé
Porto Novo
Niger
CAMEROON
Bangui
Yaoundé
Gulf of Guinea
Malabo
EQUATORIAL GUINEA
Congo Basin
Congo
UGANDA
Kampala
Lake Turkana
KENYA
Mt Kenya 5199m
Saõ Tomé
SÃO TOMÉ E PRÍNCIPE
Libreville
GABON
CONGO
Congo
Lake Victoria
RWANDA
Kigali
BURUNDI
Bujumbura
Nairobi
Kilimanjaro 5895m
Great Rift Valley
Brazzaville
DEMOCRATIC REPUBLIC OF CONGO
Kasai
Masai Steppe
INDIAN OCEAN
Cabinda (Ang.)
Kinshasa
Dodoma
SEYCHELLES
ATLANTIC OCEAN
Kwango
Lake Tanganyika
TANZANIA
Luanda
Cuango
Kasai
ANGOLA
Bié Plateau
Cubango
Zambezi
ZAMBIA
Lusaka
Lilongwe
MALAWI
Lake Malawi
Luangwa
Moroni
COMOROS
Mayotte (Fr.)
MOZAMBIQUE
Mozambique Channel
Cubango
Harare
ZIMBABWE
Zambezi
Antananarivo
Port Louis
MAURITIUS
NAMIBIA
Namib Desert
Okavango Delta
Kalahari Desert
BOTSWANA
Limpopo
MADAGASCAR
St-Denis
Réunion (Fr.)
Windhoek
Gabarone
Pretoria
Maputo
Mbabane
SWAZILAND
Vaal
Orange
LESOTHO
Maseru
Drakensberg
INDIAN OCEAN
SOUTH AFRICA
Cape Town
Cape of Good Hope

Legend
Mountain
Desert
Tundra
Cropland
Wetland
Needleleaf forest
Tropical rainforest
Temperate grassland
Ice

N

0 1000 2000 km
0 500 1000 miles

NORTHERN AFRICA

Across northern Africa stretches a string of countries – Morocco, Algeria, Tunisia, Libya and Egypt. The coasts of all five line the Mediterranean Sea. Behind these coasts lies the world's largest desert, the Sahara – a vast expanse of sand dunes, rock and gravel that bakes beneath the cloudless skies. Al Aziziyah in Libya holds the record for the world's highest temperature: 58°C in the shade.

The main cities and towns in northern Africa lie near the Mediterranean coast, or in the case of Egypt, along the mighty River Nile. The coastal areas are not as hot and arid as the desert land in the south, and there is more fertile land for growing crops.

Morocco and Algeria were once French colonies, and the French influence can be seen in the architecture of their capitals, Rabat and Algiers. However, the majority of people in northern Africa are Arabs. Their descendants conquered the region in the 8th century, bringing with them the Islamic faith.

Mountain life

In the south of Morocco lie the Atlas Mountains. The climate is cooler in this area, so children wear warmer clothes.

Plant life

The sand dunes and rocky wastelands of the Sahara deter most plants from growing, but dotted across the vast, empty desert are green oases. Each oasis has a well at its centre that taps underground reserves of fresh water. Date palms grow around the wells, sometimes in their thousands. They provide valuable shade in which vegetables can be grown. Rain falls in coastal regions and in the Atlas Mountains, which cross Morocco and Algeria. Here, farmers grow oranges, lemons, grapes and beans.

Water supplies

Northern Africa has few rivers, but it has one very famous one. The Nile snakes through Egypt to the Mediterranean Sea – a journey of 6,670 km. Farmers draw water from the river to irrigate their crops. From the air, the Nile valley looks like a green ribbon. On either side of it lies the baking desert. But underneath the desert are vast supplies of water that collected on top of layers of impermeable rock in ancient times. This water is pumped to the surface and carried across the desert by huge pipelines. In Libya, the Kufra Basin, a single underground water reserve, contains more water than the Nile produces in 220 years.

Peoples of the Nile Valley

The River Nile gave rise to one of the world's earliest civilizations in ancient Egypt, more than 5,000 years ago. But it was the Romans who brought the countries of northern Africa together, gradually conquering the entire Mediterranean coast from 146 BC.

In the 7th century AD, the Arabs swept across the region, bringing with them the religion of Islam. Almost all the people of these lands are now Muslim, and the main language is Arabic. French is also spoken in Morocco, Tunisia and Algeria, as these countries were ruled by France until the 1950s and 1960s.

Nomadic herders

The Tuareg people are nomadic Berbers who live by herding camels and goats in the desert regions of southern Algeria and Libya. Their traditional dress is made of long strips of black or blue cotton.

Everyday life

Most people in northern Africa live by farming, sea-fishing, trade or craftwork. Others work in the tourist industry, looking after the thousands of foreign visitors who come to enjoy the 'winter sun' on the beaches of Morocco and Tunisia, or to visit the sights of ancient Egypt.

In the traditional villages, people live in flat-roofed houses made with mud bricks and palm timbers. Most of the big cities are close to the coast, with busy streets crammed with cars and buses. Tall modern buildings have been built around the old quarters with their winding streets and souks (covered markets). The souks are packed with hundreds of tiny stalls selling fruit, spices, hand-woven rugs, baskets and jewellery.

Five times a day the loudspeakers in the city mosques resonate with the voices of the muezzins (religious leaders) calling Muslims to prayer. When worshippers enter a mosque, they remove their shoes and wash in the fountains before praying in the cool, shaded halls. In Morocco, mosques are adorned with pottery tiles, attached to the walls in elaborate patterns – an art form called zellij.

Head start

This young acrobat is one of many entertainers who perform in the central square of Marrakech, Morocco. Jugglers, magicians, snake charmers and storytellers also compete to catch the eye of shoppers and passers-by.

Political troubles

All the countries of northern Africa are led by presidents, except Morocco, which has a king (Mohammed VI, who succeeded to the throne in 1999). Since gaining independence from France in 1956, Tunisia has been ruled by one political party. When elections were held in 1999, the country's president, Zine El Abidine Ben Ali, won with 99 per cent of the vote and other countries were suspicious about whether this vote was rigged (manipulated dishonestly).

Libya is ruled as a strict Islamic state by a military government under Colonel Mu'ammar al-Gaddafi, who came to power in 1969. Economic sanctions were imposed on Libya by the United Nations during the 1990s because the country refused to hand over suspected terrorists to an international court for trial. The sanctions were lifted in 1999 and Libya has been developing new trade links with other countries.

Neighbouring Algeria has been a troubled country since 1991. Conflict between the ruling regime and Islamic fundamentalists has cost more than 75,000 lives. The country has the world's fourth-largest reserves of natural gas, and major deposits of oil. But the political turmoil has weakened the economy and there is high unemployment.

The difficulties of life at home have caused many people from northern Africa to seek new lives abroad, especially in France, Spain and Belgium, and in the Middle East.

The pyramids

The ancient Egyptians built the pyramids at Giza about 4,500 years ago, as tombs for their kings. Today, they attract thousands of tourists.

Entertainment

Festivals in northern Africa are big, colourful events. In Egypt, moulids (giant funfairs and religious celebrations rolled into one) are held to celebrate the birthdays of local saints or holy people. In Morocco, people travel a long way to take part in the annual Berber moussems (bride fairs) in the Atlas Mountains. At the bride fairs, Berber men and women can look for marriage partners.

Television is an increasingly popular form of entertainment, and sports such as football are widely played throughout the region.

Festival time

At the annual Fantasia festival in Morocco, villagers participate by riding their horses and firing their guns.

Football star

The Algerian-born football player Zinedine Zidane was a key player in the victorious French World Cup team in 1998, and is a popular hero in Algeria.

EASTERN AFRICA

The grasslands of Kenya and Tanzania, with their herds of zebra and wildebeest, are some of the best-known landscapes of eastern Africa. So, too, are the white sand beaches and palm trees of the Seychelles. The drier landscapes of Sudan, parts of Ethiopia, Eritrea and Somalia are tough places to live, frequently suffering droughts and famine.

Say it with beads

Masai women wear elaborate discs of beads. The number and colours of the beads show whether a woman is married and how many children she has. They also show her wealth.

The Masai

Some 300,000 Masai people live in Kenya and Tanzania, and many follow the traditional way of life, herding cattle in the grasslands. A Masai man's wealth is measured by the size of his cattle herd. Small family groups live in kraals (encampments). A hedge of thorn bush surrounds their houses, which are made of mud, dung and tree branches. Their main food is meat, milk and fresh blood, drawn from living cattle and mixed with powdered berries.

Living by the seasons

The Nuer and Dinka peoples live along the banks of the River Nile in southern Sudan, raising cattle, growing millet and fishing. When the Nile floods in the rainy season they move from the riverside to villages on higher land. In the drier north of Sudan, and in Somalia, people live as nomadic herders, while more settled villagers cluster around oases.

In Ethiopia, the land ranges between desert and the high plateaux where most Ethiopians live. Here there is enough rainfall to graze cattle and grow crops such as wheat, beans and coffee.

Deadly aim

Masai men, in their traditional red cloaks, take pride in their skills and courage as warriors. These same skills are also needed to protect their herds as they roam the grasslands.

Foreign influences

Ethiopia was the first country in Africa to adopt Christianity, in the early 4th century. Islam spread south from northern Africa after the 7th century, and was also brought to the coasts of eastern Africa by Arab traders from Yemen and Oman. The white stone towns on the islands of Zanzibar in Tanzania and Lamu in Kenya still have a noticeable Arab influence.

In the 19th and 20th centuries, Europeans took over much of eastern Africa as colonies. As well as exerting a cultural and political influence, the European colonizers turned much of the fertile land into large farms to produce crops for export. By the 1960s, the African nations had gained their independence.

Health education

A film is being made with puppets to teach people about malaria, a common disease in eastern Africa. It is caused by a germ carried by mosquitoes, which spread the disease by biting people.

The Arab dhow

This traditional sailing boat was used by Arab traders along the coast of eastern Africa 4,000 years ago. Today, dhows are used for coastal trade and as fishing boats.

Tourism

The grasslands or savanna of eastern Africa are home to a rich variety of wildlife, such as cheetahs, lions and zebra. Large areas have been set aside as national parks and game reserves, where animals are protected. Every year, many tourists visit Kenya and Tanzania to go on safari. Park rangers take them into the reserves in Land Rovers and they are able to watch the animals at close quarters. Tourism brings in much-needed foreign income and provides jobs.

Tourists also visit the coast, to enjoy the warm sea and sand. The Seychelles, a set of 115 islands off the coast of Kenya, are famous for their white sand beaches. These islands do not have much to export to the rest of the world except fish, coconut products and the spice, cinnamon. Three-quarters of their income comes from tourism.

Champion runner

Ethiopia's Derartu Tulu was first across the finishing line in the 10,000 m final at the Sydney Olympics in 2000.

Record-breakers

Eastern Africa has produced some fine athletes. The Ethiopian Miruts Yifter won both the 5,000 m and the 10,000 m races at the 1980 Olympics in Moscow. Ethiopian runner Belayneh Dinsano held the world record for the men's marathon for ten years after breaking the record in the Netherlands in 1988. The new Ethiopian hero is the 10,000 m world record holder, Haile Gebrselassie.

Kenya came to world attention at the 1968 Olympics in Mexico City, when Kip Keino won the 1,500 m and Naftali Temu won the 10,000 m race. In 1998, Kenya's Paul Tergat broke the record for the men's half-marathon in Milan, and in 1999 Tegla Loroupe broke the record for the women's marathon in Berlin.

WESTERN AFRICA

The Sahara Desert extends right across Africa. Along its southern border, it gradually becomes less dry, forming a broad band of semi-desert known as the Sahel. Farther south towards the equator, and towards the coasts, there is more rainfall and the landscape becomes greener. The River Niger flows across western Africa from Sierra Leone to Nigeria, passing through the dry landscapes of Mali on the way.

Mud brick mosques

These mosques in Djenné, Mali, are made of mud. Here, Muslim culture comes together with African building materials.

Desert–dwellers

Some countries in western Africa, such as Mali, Mauritania and Niger, are mainly desert and semi-desert. Here nomadic people such as the Tuareg of northern Niger live by herding, travelling with their camels, goats and flocks of sheep in search of pasture. The children attend school on the move, in 'tent schools'.

Other desert-dwellers have settled around oases, where they live in mud brick homes and grow dates, vegetables and grains. Life for many people is becoming harder as the Sahel gets drier and the population grows. Niger has one of the fastest growing populations in the world. Nearly half of its people are under the age of 15.

Village life

Closer to the coasts and the equator, the landscape changes to grassland and forests. The people here live in villages, in round, mud houses with roofs made of palm thatch. The women look after the household and grow maize, peanuts, yams and cassava to feed the family. The men tend herds of cattle and goats.

Much of the southern coast is lined with mangrove swamps and islands. Many people in southern Togo and Benin live in fishing villages raised above the water on stilts.

Slavery

From the 16th to the 19th century, millions of African slaves were bought by Europeans and sent to work on sugar plantations in the Caribbean and South America. They were also taken to North America to work on tobacco and cotton plantations.

Whole familes and villages were shipped to the Americas as slaves. They were treated very cruelly. Shackled in chains, they were crammed on to slave ships for the long journey across the Atlantic Ocean. Two-thirds of the slaves died on the voyage or from disease, ill-treatment and overwork when they reached the plantations.

By the time the slave trade ended in the 19th century, 12 million Africans had been shipped through the slave ports, such as Gorée in Senegal.

Fish-eaters

This Mauritanian girl is taking home fish for the family's meal. Fish is an important food on the west African coast. The Senegalese are amongst the biggest fish-eaters in the world – second only to Japan.

Football crazy

Football is played in towns and villages throughout western Africa, although there are few proper grass pitches.

Traditional ways

As in most parts of Africa, the people use a mixture of traditional and Western medicine. Many Western medicines are too expensive, and life-threatening diseases such as malaria and tuberculosis are widespread. Traditional healers, or witch doctors, are honoured, and sometimes feared, members of the community. The neem tree has been used by witch doctors for hundreds of years for its remarkable medicinal powers and is now being tested by international pharmaceutical companies.

The old tribal religions based on ancestor worship are still practised alongside Islam and Christianity. In the traditional masquerade, performers disguised from head to foot in robes and an elaborate mask dance and act out stories about the spirits and ancestors.

Funeral dance

A funeral is an occasion for traditional ceremonies and dancing. These masked Dogon dancers are performing at a funeral in Mali.

Most people remain loyal to their tribe and speak a local language, such as Hausa and Ibo in Nigeria and Mossi in Burkina Faso. Many tribes are still ruled by powerful chiefs. The Asante of Ghana, for example, have the Asantehene as their chief. He attends ceremonies wearing spectacular robes and a gold crown, and sits on a gold throne. In Mali, the chiefs have griots (their own musical entertainers), who write songs about tribal history. Traditional musicians in western Africa play a kora, which looks like a lute or guitar and sounds like a harp.

City life

The larger cities of western Africa have modern high-rise office blocks and shopping malls. Wealthy people enjoy comfortable lives, with air-conditioned homes, satellite television, computers and hi-tech audio equipment. Their children often go on to university and many study abroad.

But for the vast majority of people, life is not like that at all. They live in the sprawling suburbs, in small apartments or shacks, often without running water or electricity. Most children go to primary schools, which are free, but many receive little further education as their parents are too poor to pay the secondary school fees.

Street vendor
In the cities some people scratch a living by selling cigarettes, matches, shoelaces or, like this boy, toothpaste.

Arts and crafts

Western Africa has a proud arts and crafts tradition. The craftsmen of the old kingdom of Benin were famous for their bronze casting, and this skill is used today to make copperware and brass. An even more ancient skill was carving ivory. But now that it is illegal to kill elephants for their ivory tusks, craftsmen use wood for their intricately carved boxes and sculptures.

In the past, jewellery and masks were designed for traditional ceremonies, but today they are more likely to be sold to tourists. Craft goods made for the tourist markets range from elaborate traditional baskets to toy models of motorbikes made of bent wire.

A particularly popular product is the 'articulated chair', a low, throne-like portable chair made of two pieces of carved wood that slot together ingeniously.

West African painting is colourful and lively and often depicts daily life in a humorous way.

Political troubles

In recent years, Sierra Leone and Liberia have been torn apart by vicious civil wars. As a result of these troubles, Sierra Leone has one of the lowest life expectancies in the world. The average life expectancy is just 36 for men and 39 for women.

Most countries in western Africa are ruled as republics. The president and government are elected by the people, but the elections are not always free and fair. Ethnic loyalties are also important and often the cause of conflict.

In recent years, the Nigerian army has stepped in to take over power in their country. Many countries in western Africa, including Ghana, Côte d'Ivoire, Burkina Faso, Mauritania and Gambia, have also had military governments.

But there are signs of change in some countries. After many years of military rule, Ghana had free elections in the 1990s and now has a multi-party democracy.

Giant puppets

In Mali, masked dancers take part in a ritual performed by most of the village in June, before the arrival of the rains. This colourful giant puppet conceals several performers.

CENTRAL AFRICA

Much of central Africa lies on the equator, where it is hot and there is plenty of rain. With the exception of Chad, which spreads across the semi-desert of the Sahel into the Sahara, the land is covered with rainforest or grassland. The Democratic Republic of Congo is crossed by rivers and dotted with lakes. The east side rises up to mountains and the small countries of Rwanda and Burundi.

Pygmies

The Mbuti pygmies live in the rainforests of the Democratic Republic of Congo. The men hunt for wild animals using poisoned arrows. The women collect roots, berries and wild plants. The average height of the men is 134 cm and the women average 124 cm.

Self-sufficiency

These pygmy children are enjoying a meal that they have just prepared. The children learn at a very early age how to construct their own conical huts and how to build fires.

Natural resources

In the north of Chad, nomads shepherd their sheep and goats across the parched land in search of grazing. In the more fertile south, and in the Central African Republic, non-nomadic farmers grow maize, peppers, tomatoes, okra and cassava.

Cattle are raised in the region's grasslands and smoked beef is a very popular dish in these areas. Caterpillars are also eaten throughout central Africa as a delicacy.

Many countries in central Africa are rich in natural resources, including diamonds, copper, iron, bauxite, manganese, uranium and timber. In addition to minerals, Gabon has oil supplies, which has made it one of the richest countries in Africa.

Gabon's wealth has helped it maintain a stable government. While it is a multi-party democracy, poorer countries in the region have suffered from political unrest.

Independence and turmoil

In the late 19th century, Europeans took large areas of central Africa as colonies. They helped themselves to raw materials, such as timber and copper, to use in industries back home, and forced Africans to work on their plantations.

In the 1960s and 1970s, all the countries of central Africa won their independence. This often happened quickly, leaving weak systems of government that could be taken over by tyrants.

The Central African Republic was ruled by Jean Bedel Bokassa from 1966 to 1979. He proclaimed himself 'emperor' and had a golden throne decorated with an eagle. He spent a large fortune on himself and on his grand coronation. Bokassa was overthrown after his imperial guard massacred 100 schoolchildren who protested against being forced to wear school uniform.

The Democratic Republic of Congo was ruled by President Mobutu Sese Seko for 32 years. He lived a life of great luxury while his country lacked basic healthcare. After he was removed from power in 1997, civil war broke out and several African countries sent troops to support the government or the rebels.

Hutus and Tutsis

Rwanda and neighbouring Burundi have two main groups, the Hutu and the Tutsi. Both countries have suffered from outbursts of savagery as one tribe attacked another.

Violence erupted in Burundi in 1993 when a Hutu was elected president after decades of domination by the minority Tutsi. The new president was assassinated and thousands were killed during the political crisis.

In 1994, the Rwandan Hutus rose up after the death of their president in a mysterious plane crash, and massacred about half of all the Tutsis living in Rwanda. The rest fled, and later fought back and seized power from the Hutus. A million Rwandans died in this turmoil.

Manganese mine
Manganese is an important export in Gabon. It is used in the manufacture of steel.

Refugees

The troubles in Rwanda have left many people without a home. These Tutsi children playing on a tree live in a refugee camp in Niashishi, south Rwanda. More than 8,000 refugees live in the camp under French protection.

SOUTHERN AFRICA

The southern tip of Africa is an area of contrasts. It includes the cascades of the Victoria Falls, the dry Kalahari Desert, the plateau of Table Mountain and the unique wildlife of Madagascar. It is also a region rich in mineral deposits. The region's wealthiest country, South Africa, is the world's top producer of gold and diamonds.

Hard at work in the fields

Women in southern Africa usually cultivate the crops because most men work in industry. Young children spend the day in the fields with their mother, sometimes strapped to her back.

Gold and diamond mining

Gold and diamonds account for about one-third of South Africa's export earnings. Diamonds were first discovered in 1867 near the River Orange. A few years later, a huge diamond field was found at Kimberley. Diamonds look very plain when they are dug out of the rock. They only glitter and sparkle after expert cutting and polishing, and this is often done abroad. Gold deposits have been mined in South Africa since the 19th century. However, ore supplies are gradually diminishing and the economy is becoming less dependent on the mining industry.

Apartheid

In 1948 'apartheid' laws were passed in South Africa to keep black Africans, coloureds (mixed race) and Asians apart from whites. The laws applied to work, education, housing, public transport and entertainment. Leaders of the anti-apartheid African National Congress (ANC), including Nelson Mandela, were put in prison. Apartheid was criticized by the rest of the world and many countries stopped trading with South Africa. A sporting and entertainment ban was also enforced.

Drilling for gold

This miner is using a drill to extract the gold-bearing rock from a mine near Johannesburg.

Eventually, the all-white government realized that the country could not continue in this way. In 1990, President F W de Klerk scrapped apartheid and released Mandela from prison. In the elections of 1994, the black majority was allowed to vote for the first time. The ANC was voted into power and Mandela was elected president.

Huge changes have taken place in South Africa since 1994, but it has also been a difficult time. People of all ethnic groups have been encouraged to talk about, but also forgive, the crimes of the apartheid era, in the hope that all people can live and work together in peace. Many of its black citizens, after years of living in poverty, had high hopes that a better life would come quickly. They have been disappointed, and crime has risen sharply as a result. But hope remains that South Africa can work as a modern industrial country with opportunities for all its citizens.

The fight for independence

The other countries of southern Africa have struggled to gain their independence from European colonizers. In Zimbabwe, white settlers took power in 1965 and declared independence from Britain. They fought a long and bitter civil war with black African rebels. Rebel leader Robert Mugabe eventually took power. But violence flared again from the late 1990s when President Mugabe began to confiscate land owned by white farmers.

A communist government took over in Mozambique, but it had to fight a civil war with guerrilla forces backed by South Africa and Zimbabwe. Peace finally came in 1992. Namibia was last to gain independence, in 1990 – but only after a long armed struggle against South African control.

Black leader

Nelson Mandela was president of South Africa from 1994 to 1999. He encouraged forgiveness for those who imposed apartheid.

A cultural inheritance

Over the past 100 years, more and more people in southern Africa have moved to the towns in search of jobs. Even so, two-thirds of the people in the region still live in the countryside, in small villages of grass-thatched, mud houses. Here they grow cereals, such as sorghum and maize, as well as beans and sweet potatoes. Often the electricity supply is unreliable – at night, small lamps burn paraffin or kerosene, and wood provides heat for cooking. Some children have to walk long distances every day just to get to school.

The oldest inhabitants of the region are the San people, who have been living in the stony Kalahari Desert of Namibia and Botswana for 30,000 years. Much of their land has now been encroached on by international mining and agricultural corporations. However, some of the San people still survive by hunting for meat, gathering wild roots and berries, and storing water in ostrich egg shells.

Music and dance play a major part in the cultural life of southern Africa. Drumming is traditional at Zulu festivals in South Africa. In Mozambique, the influence of the country's former Portuguese rulers can be heard in the rhythms of the guitar. And throughout southern Africa, you can hear a very unusual instrument, the 'thumb piano'. It consists of a small, wooden, hand-held sound-box with a row of metal prongs, and produces twanging notes that are used as an accompaniment to singing.

The two tiny countries of Lesotho and Swaziland (Africa's smallest state) are both monarchies. Coronations and royal marriages are celebrated with drumming and warrior dances. The king of Swaziland's most important job is to bless the harvest. Every year, at the festival of Incwala, the king emerges from his palace to perform a ritual dance before his people. He then takes a bite of food, signalling for the feasting to begin.

Art house

Folk art is not confined to museums, it is part of everyday life in southern Africa. The Ndebele women paint the outside of their homes with bright geometric patterns.

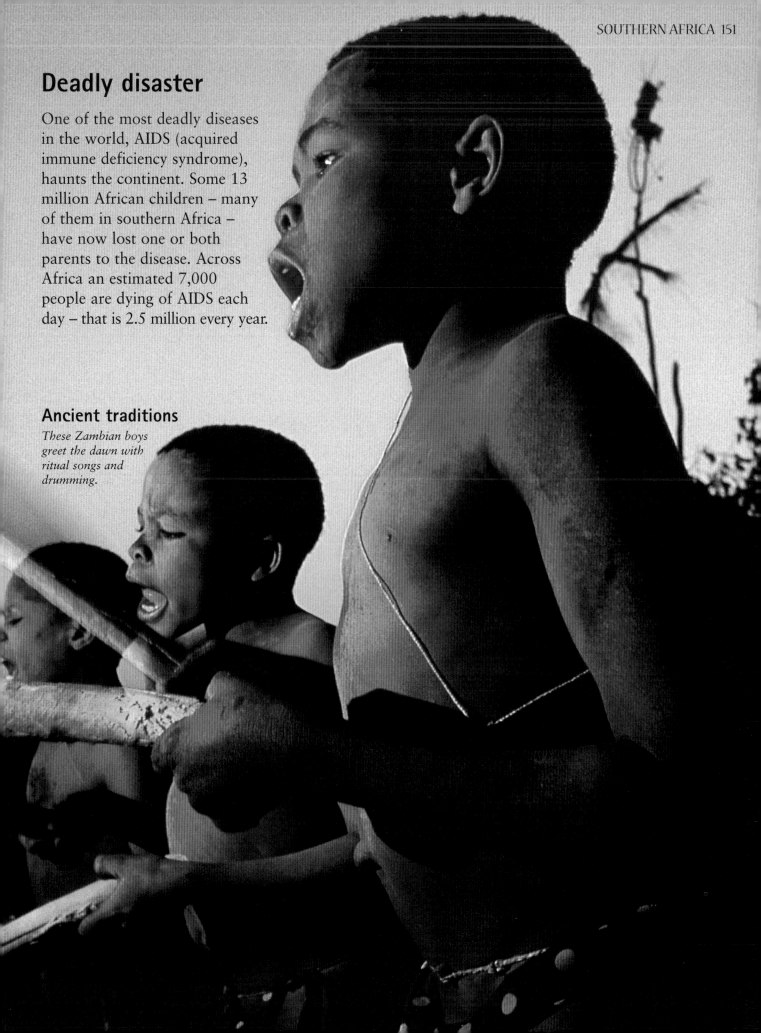

Deadly disaster

One of the most deadly diseases in the world, AIDS (acquired immune deficiency syndrome), haunts the continent. Some 13 million African children – many of them in southern Africa – have now lost one or both parents to the disease. Across Africa an estimated 7,000 people are dying of AIDS each day – that is 2.5 million every year.

Ancient traditions

These Zambian boys greet the dawn with ritual songs and drumming.

ALGERIA

Capital
Algiers
Area
2,381,741 km²
Population
30,774,000
Population density
13 per km²
Life expectancy
65 (m); 66 (f)
Religion
Islam
Languages
Arabic, French, Berber
Adult literacy rate
62 per cent
Currency
Algerian dinar

 ANGOLA

Capital
Luanda
Area
1,246,700 km²
Population
12,479,000
Population density
10 per km²
Life expectancy
45 (m); 48 (f)
Religions
Christianity, traditional beliefs
Languages
Portuguese, Umbundo,
Kimbundo, Chokwe, Ganguela
Adult literacy rate
42 per cent
Currency
new kwanza

 BENIN

Capital
Porto-Novo
Area
112,622 km²
Population
6,059,000
Population density
54 per km²
Life expectancy
51 (m); 56 (f)
Religions
Christianity, Islam, traditional
beliefs
Languages
French, Bariba, Fulani, Fon,
Yoruba
Adult literacy rate
37 per cent
Currency
CFA franc

 BOTSWANA

Capital
Gaborone
Area
581,730 km²
Population
1,611,000
Population density
3 per km²
Life expectancy
56 (m); 62 (f)
Religions
Christianity, traditional beliefs
Languages
English, Setswana
Adult literacy rate
70 per cent
Currency
pula

BURKINA-FASO

Capital
Ouagadougou
Area
274,200 km²
Population
11,616,000
Population density
39 per km²
Life expectancy
45 (m); 47 (f)
Religions
Islam, Christianity, traditional
beliefs
Languages
French, Mossi and local
languages
Adult literacy rate
19 per cent
Currency
CFA franc

 **BURUNDI**

Capital
Bujumbura
Area
27,834 km²
Population
6,483,000
Population density
226 per km²
Life expectancy
43 (m); 46 (f)
Religions
Christianity, traditional beliefs
Languages
French, Kirundi, Swahili
Adult literacy rate
35 per cent
Currency
Burundi franc

CAMEROON

Capital
Yaoundé
Area
475,442 km²
Population
14,693,000
Population density
30 per km²
Life expectancy
53 (m); 56 (f)
Religions
Christianity, Islam, traditional beliefs
Languages
English, French and local languages
Adult literacy rate
63 per cent
Currency
CFA franc

 CAPE VERDE

Capital
Praia
Area
4,033 km²
Population
418,000
Population density
104 per km²
Life expectancy
64 (m); 71 (f)
Religion
Christianity
Languages
Portuguese, Creole
Adult literacy rate
72 per cent
Currency
Cape Verdean escudo

 **CENTRAL AFRICAN REPUBLIC**

Capital
Bangui
Area
622,984 km²
Population
3,550,000
Population density
6 per km²
Life expectancy
47 (m); 52 (f)
Religions
Christianity, traditional beliefs
Languages
French, Sango
Adult literacy rate
60 per cent
Currency
CFA franc

 CHAD

Capital
N'Djamena
Area
1,284,000 km²
Population
7,458,000
Population density
6 per km²
Life expectancy
45 (m); 51 (f)
Religions
Islam, Christianity, traditional beliefs
Languages
French, Arabic and local languages
Adult literacy rate
48 per cent
Currency
CFA franc

 COMOROS

Capital
Moroni, on Grande Comore (Njazidja)
Area
1,862 km²
Population
676,000
Population density
354 per km²
Life expectancy
55 (m); 56 (f)
Religion
Islam
Languages
Comorian (Swahili and Arabic), French, Arabic
Adult literacy rate
57 per cent
Currency
Comoros franc

DEMOCRATIC REPUBLIC OF CONGO

Capital
Kinshasa
Area
2,344,885 km²
Population
50,335,000
Population density
21 per km²
Life expectancy
50 (m); 54 (f)
Religions
Christianity, Islam, traditional beliefs
Languages
French, Lingala, Kingwana, Tshiluba and local languages
Adult literacy rate
77 per cent
Currency
Congolese franc

DJIBOUTI

Capital
Djibouti
Area
23,200 km²
Population
629,000
Population density
27 per km²
Life expectancy
47 (m); 50 (f)
Religions
Islam, Christianity
Languages
Arabic, French
Adult literacy rate
46 per cent
Currency
Djibouti franc

 EGYPT

Capital
Cairo
Area
997,738 km²
Population
67,226,000
Population density
66 per km²
Life expectancy
63 (m); 66 (f)
Religions
Islam, Christianity
Languages
Arabic, English, French
Adult literacy rate
51 per cent
Currency
Egyptian pound

 **EQUATORIAL GUINEA**

Capital
Malabo
Area
28,051 km²
Population
442,000
Population density
15 per km²
Life expectancy
46 (m); 50 (f)
Religion
Christianity
Languages
Spanish, French, Fang and local languages
Adult literacy rate
78 per cent
Currency
CFA franc

 ERITREA

Capital
Asmara
Area
121,144 km²
Population
3,719,000
Population density
31 per km²
Life expectancy
48 (m); 51 (f)
Religions
Islam, Christianity
Languages
Arabic, Tigre, English
Adult literacy rate
20 per cent
Currency
nakfa

 ETHIOPIA

Capital
Addis Ababa
Area
1,133,380 km²
Population
61,672,000
Population density
53 per km²
Life expectancy
46 (m); 49 (f)
Religions
Christianity, Islam, traditional beliefs
Languages
Arharic, English and local languages
Adult literacy rate
35 per cent
Currency
birr

 GABON

Capital
Libreville
Area
267,667 km²
Population
1,385,000
Population density
4 per km²
Life expectancy
52 (m); 55 (f)
Religions
Christianity, traditional beliefs
Languages
French, Fang, Bantu dialects
Adult literacy rate
63 per cent
Currency
CFA franc

GAMBIA

Capital
Banjul
Area
11,295 km²
Population
1,385,000
Population density
109 per km²
Life expectancy
43 (m); 47 (f)
Religion
Islam
Languages
English, Mandinka, Fula,
Wolof and other local
languages
Adult literacy rate
39 per cent
Currency
dalasi

 GHANA

Capital
Accra
Area
238,537 km²
Population
19,678,000
Population density
80 per km²
Life expectancy
54 (m); 58 (f)
Religions
Christianity, Islam, traditional
beliefs
Languages
English and local languages
Adult literacy rate
64 per cent
Currency
cedi

 GUINEA

Capital
Conakry
Area
245,857 km²
Population
7,360,000
Population density
30 per km²
Life expectancy
44 (m); 45 (f)
Religions
Islam, traditional beliefs
Languages
French, Soussou, Manika and
other local languages
Adult literacy rate
36 per cent
Currency
Guinean franc

 GUINEA-BISSAU

Capital
Bissau
Area
36,125 km²
Population
1,187,000
Population density
32 per km²
Life expectancy
41 (m); 44 (f)
Religions
Islam, Christianity,
traditional beliefs
Languages
Portuguese, Creole
Adult literacy rate
55 per cent
Currency
CFA franc

 IVORY COAST

Capital
Yamoussoukro
Area
322,462 km²
Population
14,526,000
Population density
44 per km²
Life expectancy
50 (m); 54 (f)
Religions
Islam, Christianity, traditional
beliefs
Languages
French and local languages
Adult literacy rate
40 per cent
Currency
CFA franc

KENYA

Capital
Nairobi
Area
580,367 km²
Population
29,549,000
Population density
50 per km²
Life expectancy
57 (m); 61 (f)
Religions
Christianity, Islam, traditional
beliefs
Languages
Kiswahili, English, Kikuyu,
Luo
Adult literacy rate
78 per cent
Currency
Kenyan shilling

LESOTHO

Capital
Maseru
Area
30,355 km²
Population
2,108,000
Population density
68 per km²
Life expectancy
56 (m); 59 (f)
Religion
Christianity
Languages
English, Sesotho
Adult literacy rate
71 per cent
Currency
loti

 LIBERIA

Capital
Monrovia
Area
97,754 km²
Population
2,930,000
Population density
27 per km²
Life expectancy
54 (m); 57 (f)
Religions
Christianity, Islam
Languages
English and many local
languages
Adult literacy rate
38 per cent
Currency
Liberian dollar

 LIBYA

Capital
Tripoli
Area
1,775,500 km²
Population
5,471,000
Population density
3 per km²
Life expectancy
62 (m); 65 (f)
Religion
Islam
Languages
Arabic, English, Italian
Adult literacy rate
76 per cent
Currency
Libyan dinar

 MADAGASCAR

Capital
Antananarivo
Area
587,041 km²
Population
15,497,000
Population density
26 per km²
Life expectancy
55 (m); 58 (f)
Religions
Christianity, traditional beliefs
Languages
Malagasy, French, Hova and
other local languages
Adult literacy rate
46 per cent
Currency
Malagasy franc

 MALAWI

Capital
Lilongwe
Area
118,484 km²
Population
10,640,000
Population density
87 per km²
Life expectancy
43 (m); 46 (f)
Religions
Christianity, Islam, traditional
beliefs
Languages
English, Chichewa and other
local languages
Adult literacy rate
56 per cent
Currency
Malawian kwacha

 MALI

Capital
Bamako
Area
1,240,192 km²
Population
10,960,000
Population density
9 per km²
Life expectancy
55 (m); 58 (f)
Religions
Islam, traditional beliefs
Languages
French and 12 other official
languages
Adult literacy rate
31 per cent
Currency
CFA franc

MAURITANIA

Capital
Nouakchott
Area
1,030,700 km^2
Population
2,598,000
Population density
2 per km^2
Life expectancy
50 (m); 53 (f)
Religion
Islam
Languages
Arabic, French and local
languages
Adult literacy rate
38 per cent
Currency
ouguiya

 MAURITIUS

Capital
Port Louis
Area
2,040 km^2
Population
1,174,000
Population density
569 per km^2
Life expectancy
66 (m); 74 (f)
Religions
Christianity, Hinduism, Islam
Languages
English, Creole, French and
several Indian and Chinese
dialects
Adult literacy rate
83 per cent
Currency
Mauritian rupee

 MOROCCO

Capital
Rabat
Area
710,850 km^2
Population
28,238,000
Population density
39 per km^2
Life expectancy
62 (m); 66 (f)
Religion
Islam
Languages
Arabic, Berber, Spanish,
French
Adult literacy rate
44 per cent
Currency
Moroccan dirham

 MOZAMBIQUE

Capital
Maputo
Area
799,380 km^2
Population
17,299,000
Population density
21 per km^2
Life expectancy
44 (m); 47 (f)
Religions
Christianity, Islam, traditional
beliefs
Languages
Portuguese and local languages
Adult literacy rate
40 per cent
Currency
metical

 NAMIBIA

Capital
Windhoek
Area
824,292 km^2
Population
1,695,000
Population density
2 per km^2
Life expectancy
54 (m); 57 (f)
Religion
Christianity
Languages
English, Afrikaans, German
and local languages
Adult literacy rate
62 per cent
Currency
Namibian dollar

NIGER

Capital
Niamey
Area
1,267,000 km^2
Population
10,400,000
Population density
8 per km^2
Life expectancy
45 (m); 48 (f)
Religion
Islam
Languages
French and local languages
Adult literacy rate
14 per cent
Currency
CFA franc

NIGERIA

Capital
Abuja
Area
923,768 km²
Population
126,636,000
Population density
115 per km²
Life expectancy
49 (m); 52 (f)
Religions
Islam, Christianity, traditional beliefs
Languages
English, Hausa, Yoruba, Ibo
Adult literacy rate
57 per cent
Currency
naira

 **REPUBLIC OF CONGO**

Capital
Brazzaville
Area
342,000 km²
Population
2,864,000
Population density
8 per km²
Life expectancy
48 (m); 54 (f)
Religions
Christianity, Islam, traditional beliefs
Languages
French, Kikongo, Lingala and other local languages
Adult literacy rate
75 per cent
Currency
CFA franc

 **RWANDA**

Capital
Kigali
Area
26,338 km²
Population
7,235,000
Population density
251 per km²
Life expectancy
45 (m); 48 (f)
Religions
Christianity, Islam, traditional beliefs
Languages
French, English, Kinyarwanda, Kiswahili
Adult literacy rate
60 per cent
Currency
Rwanda franc

 **SAO TOMÉ E PRINCIPE**

Capital
Sao Tomé
Area
1,001 km²
Population
144,000
Population density
140 per km²
Life expectancy
67 (m); 67 (f)
Religions
Christianity, traditional beliefs
Languages
Portuguese and local languages
Adult literacy rate
25 per cent
Currency
dobra

 SENEGAL

Capital
Dakar
Area
196,722 km²
Population
9,279,000
Population density
47 per km²
Life expectancy
48 (m); 50 (f)
Religion
Islam
Languages
French and local languages
Adult literacy rate
33 per cent
Currency
CFA franc

 SEYCHELLES

Capital
Victoria, on Mahé
Area
454 km²
Population
80,000
Population density
176 per km²
Life expectancy
65 (m); 74 (f)
Religion
Christianity
Languages
Creole, English, French
Adult literacy rate
85 per cent
Currency
Seychelles rupee

SIERRA LEONE

Capital
Freetown
Area
71,740 km^2
Population
4,717,000
Population density
64 per km^2
Life expectancy
32 (m); 36 (f)
Religions
Islam, Christianity, traditional beliefs
Languages
English, Mende, Temne, Krio (Creole)
Adult literacy rate
31 per cent
Currency
leone

 SOMALIA

Capital
Mogadishu
Area
637,657 km^2
Population
9,240,000
Population density
14 per km^2
Life expectancy
45 (m); 49 (f)
Religion
Islam
Languages
Somali, Arabic, English, Italian
Adult literacy rate
24 per cent
Currency
Somali shilling

 SOUTH AFRICA

Capital cities
Pretoria (administrative),
Cape Town (legislative),
Bloemfontein (judicial)
Area
1,219,080 km^2
Population
43,054,000
Population density
35 per km^2
Life expectancy
60 (m); 66 (f)
Religions
Christianity, Hinduism, Islam,
Languages
Afrikaans, English and nine
African languages
Adult literacy rate
82 per cent
Currency
rand

 SUDAN

Capital
Khartoum
Area
2,505,813 km^2
Population
28,883,000
Population density
12 per km^2
Life expectancy
49 (m); 52 (f)
Religions
Islam, Christianity, traditional beliefs
Languages
Arabic, English and local languages
Adult literacy rate
46 per cent
Currency
Sudanese dinar

 **SWAZILAND**

Capital
Mbabane
Area
17,363 km^2
Population
980,000
Population density
55 per km^2
Life expectancy
55 (m); 60 (f)
Religions
Christianity, traditional beliefs
Languages
English, Siswati
Adult literacy rate
77 per cent
Currency
lilangeni

TANZANIA

Capital
Dodoma
Area
945,087 km^2
Population
32,793,000
Population density
34 per km^2
Life expectancy
52 (m); 55 (f)
Religions
Islam, Christianity, traditional beliefs
Languages
Kiswahili, English and local languages
Adult literacy rate
68 per cent
Currency
Tanzanian shilling

TOGO

Capital
Lomé
Area
56,785 km²
Population
4,512,000
Population density
77 per km²
Life expectancy
49 (m); 52 (f)
Religions
Christianity, Islam, traditional beliefs
Languages
French, Kabiye, Ewe and other local languages
Adult literacy rate
52 per cent
Currency
CFA franc

 TUNISIA

Capital
Tunis
Area
163,610 km²
Population
9,457,000
Population density
57 per km²
Life expectancy
69 (m); 73 (f)
Religion
Islam
Languages
Arabic, Berber, French
Adult literacy rate
67 per cent
Currency
Tunisian dinar

 **UGANDA**

Capital
Kampala
Area
241,139 km²
Population
21,620,000
Population density
87 per km²
Life expectancy
40 (m); 42 (f)
Religions
Christianity, Islam
Languages
English, Luganda and local languages
Adult literacy rate
62 per cent
Currency
Ugandan shilling

 ZAMBIA

Capital
Lusaka
Area
752,614 km²
Population
10,407,000
Population density
14 per km²
Life expectancy
37 (m); 37 (f)
Religions
Christianity, traditional beliefs
Languages
English, Bemba, Kaonda, Lozi, Tonga and other local languages
Adult literacy rate
78 per cent
Currency
Zambian kwacha

 ZIMBABWE

Capital
Harare
Area
390,759 km²
Population
13,079,000
Population density
32 per km²
Life expectancy
58 (m); 62 (f)
Religions
Christianity, traditional beliefs
Languages
English, Chishona, Sindebele and other local languages
Adult literacy rate
85 per cent
Currency
Zimbabwe dollar

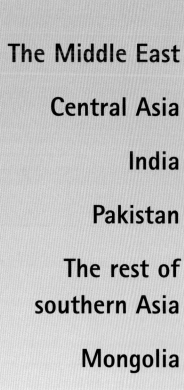

ASIA

Severnaya
Zemlya

Kara
Sea

Taymyr
Peninsula

Yamal
Peninsula

Gydan
Peninsula

Central
Siberian
Plateau

West
Siberian
Plain

Ob'

Irtysh

Yenisey

Ural Mountains

RUSSIAN
FEDERATION

(Capital Moscow)

Black Sea

ANKARA

TURKEY

GEORGIA

Astana

KAZAKHSTAN

Altai

Ulan Bat

MONGOLI

CYPRUS
Nicosia

T'bilisi
ARMENIA
Yerevan

AZERBAIJAN
Baku

Caspian Sea

Aral
Sea

Lake
Balkhash

LEBANON
Beirut
Jerusalem
ISRAEL
JORDAN

Damascus
SYRIA
Amman

Tigris

Euphrates

Baghdad

TURKMENISTAN

Ashgabat

UZBEKISTAN

Tashkent

Bishkek
KYRGYZSTAN

Tian Shan

Pik Pobedy
7440m

Gobi
Deser

IRAQ

TEHRAN

IRAN

Dushanbe
TAJIKISTAN

Taklimakan

KUWAIT

Iranian
Plateau

Hindu Kush

Kabul

KASHMIR
Administered
by Pakistan

K2
8611m

Kunlun Shan

Kuwait

The Gulf

AFGHANISTAN

Islamabad

AKSAI
Administered
by China

CHINA

Riyadh

Al Manamah
BAHRAIN
Doha

PAKISTAN

Plateau
of Tibet

Red Sea

SAUDI
ARABIA

QATAR
Abu Dhabi
UAE

Muscat

Indus

Thar Desert

New
Delhi

HIMALAYA

Mt. Everest
8848m

Kuntun Shan

Sana

Arabian
Peninsula

OMAN

NEPAL
Kathmandu

Thimphu
BHUTAN

Brahmaputra

YEMEN

Ganges

BANGLADESH

Gulf of Aden

Socotra

Arabian
Sea

INDIA

Dhaka

Irrawaddy

MYANMAR

LAOS

Deccan
Plateau

Bay of
Bengal

Vientiane

THAILAN

Yangoon
(Rangoon)

Bangkol

Laccadive
Is.

Andaman
Is.

Andaman
Sea

CAMP
Phnom Pe

Gulf of
Thailand

SRI LANKA
Colombo

MALDIVES

Nicobar
Is.

Male

INDIAN

OCEAN

MALAYSIA
Kuala Lumpur

Singapore

Sumatra

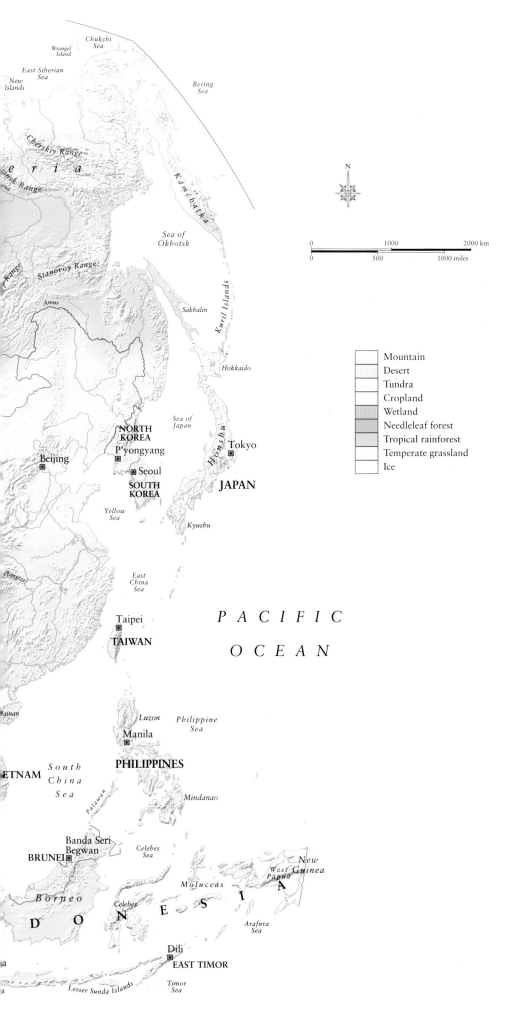

Wrangel Island
Chukchi Sea
East Siberian Sea
New Islands
Bering Sea

Cherskiy Range

Kamchatka

Stanovoy Range

Sea of Okhotsk

Amur

Sakhalin

Kuril Islands

Hokkaido

NORTH KOREA
P'yongyang

Beijing

□ Seoul
SOUTH KOREA

Sea of Japan

Honshu

Tokyo

JAPAN

Yellow Sea

Kyushu

Yangtze

East China Sea

Taipei
TAIWAN

P A C I F I C

O C E A N

Hainan

Luzon

Philippine Sea

Manila

PHILIPPINES

ETNAM

South China Sea

Palawan

Mindanao

Banda Seri Begwan
BRUNEI

Celebes Sea

Moluccas

West Papua

New Guinea

Borneo

D O N E S I A

Celebes

Arafura Sea

Dili
EAST TIMOR

Lesser Sunda Islands

Timor Sea

N

0   1000   2000 km
0   500   1000 miles

- Mountain
- Desert
- Tundra
- Cropland
- Wetland
- Needleleaf forest
- Tropical rainforest
- Temperate grassland
- Ice

Ring of fire

Japan lies on the Pacific 'ring of fire', making it vulnerable to volcanic eruptions, earthquakes and tsunamis.

Financial city

The Chinese city of Hong Kong was under British rule until 1997 when it was returned to China. It is a financial centre with major world banks and is China's most crowded city.

India

The Indian subcontinent is separated from the rest of Asia by the Himalayas. India is the world's second most populous country after China. The USA is the third most populous.

Oil rich

Middle East countries, such as Saudi Arabia and Kuwait, have huge gas and oil reserves which they export.

Western and southern Asia
THE MIDDLE EAST

The world's first cities grew up about 5,500 years ago in the area between the Tigris and Euphrates rivers. This region, called Mesopotamia, lies mainly in what is now Iraq. Much of the land is dry, but these early civilizations dug irrigation canals to direct the river water onto their crops. Water is still a precious commodity – perhaps more precious even than oil, which has brought great wealth to many countries in the region.

Camel racing

Today, camels are more likely to be bred for racing than as beasts of burden. A big race at Dubai's racetrack may have up to 50 runners. To keep the weight down, the jockeys are usually young boys.

The Bedouin

A large area of southern Saudi Arabia is known as the 'Empty Quarter' because it contains little but shifting sand dunes. It is one of the most hostile environments on earth, but the Bedouin can survive there. This would be impossible but for their camels, which can travel for two weeks without eating or drinking. The camels carry all the Bedouin's supplies, including tents, rugs and bedding, skins full of water, and food, such as bread, dates and goats' cheese. The camels provide milk to drink and to make into yoghurt. They also supply meat, wool, leather and dung to burn as fuel. The Bedouin move around the desert with their flocks of sheep and herds of goats, using their skills to find pasture and vital water-holes.

Oases

Wherever there is sufficient water, settlements have sprung up in the desert, allowing people to populate and grow dates, pumpkins, onions and figs. They also grow wheat, which is used to make flat bread. Goats and chickens are raised for food – but not pigs, because pork is forbidden by Islam.

Some oases are huge. Riyadh, the capital and largest city of Saudi Arabia with a population of 1.8 million, is an oasis. So, too, is Damascus, the capital of Syria, the world's oldest continuously inhabited city, dating back some 4,500 years.

Mountain farmers

Not all of the land in the Middle East is desert. Where there are hills and mountains, there is usually enough rainfall to turn the landscape green. Most of the people of Yemen live in the hills that line the Red Sea coast in the west. Here they can grow wheat, vegetables, cotton and coffee.

Much of Lebanon is mountainous. The best farmland is in the hills, and in the Bekaa Valley in the Lebanon Mountains. All kinds of vegetables can be grown here, such as onions, tomatoes and aubergines, as well as citrus fruits, olives and almonds. In the Elburz Mountains of northern Iran, the rivers are lined with ribbons of green farmland, but the summer heat creates bare, rocky desert wherever the land is beyond the reach of water.

Summers are hot throughout the region, and a big problem facing farmers is drought. The heat evaporates water before plants can absorb it. For every litre absorbed by plants, five litres may evaporate into the air.

Three world religions

The region at the eastern end of the Mediterranean, covering Israel and Syria, is known as the Holy Land to Jews and Christians. It includes Canaan, the 'promised land' of Abraham, where most of the events of the Old Testament took place. Israel is where Jesus was born and preached his message. Islam developed in the west of Saudi Arabia, in the Prophet Muhammad's home city of Mecca and the city of Medina, 350 km to the north of Mecca. After Muhammad's death in AD 632, his followers spread Islam far and wide, mainly by conquest. As a result, Islam is now the main religion, and Arabic the main language of the Middle East.

Islam is divided into two main branches – Shiism and Sunnism. Most Muslims are Sunnis, but the Iranians are Shiites. A revolution led by Ayatollah Khomeini overthrew the rule of the Shah (king) in 1979. Since then, the Islamic government of Iran has applied a strict interpretation of Islamic law, restricting the Western style of life that developed during the Shah's reign. Women could no longer be seen in public in jeans, for example, and had to cover themselves in a chador (a black, hooded robe).

The Torah

These Jews are carrying a copy of the Torah, a hand-written scroll containing the laws of Judaism.

The Diaspora

Although Israel is the Jewish Holy Land, most Jews were pushed out in ancient times. They were made to settle abroad by foreign conquerors such as the Romans. This scattering of the nation was called the Diaspora. In the 19th century, Jews began lobbying for the

Protest march

These Palestinian children carry portraits of Palestinian leader Yasser Arafat and 14-year-old Alaa Jawabreh, who was killed by gunfire in a refugee camp near Hebron in 2000.

creation of a new Jewish state in what was then called Palestine. Jewish settlers returned to these lands, and after World War II they fought for their own nation, declaring an independent state of Israel in 1948. This went against the wishes of the Muslim Palestinians already living there. Four wars followed as neighbouring Arab countries tried to force out the Jews in favour of the Palestinians, but they failed each time.

In 1994, the Palestinians were given limited self-rule over parts of the West Bank (of the River Jordan) and the Gaza Strip (along the Mediterranean coast). But many Palestinians still fight for a better settlement.

This on-going struggle remains the greatest cause of friction in the Middle East and throughout the Muslim world.

Turkish mosque

This mosque in southern Turkey looks out over the landscape of Syria. Modern Turkey does not have a state religion. But it was once a strictly Muslim country and recently there has been a revival of interest in Islamic culture.

A precious resource

The lack of water has always been a problem for the Middle East. In the past, ingenious systems were developed to transport it across the land. In Iran, foggaras (large tunnels) were dug beneath the desert to bring water to oases from mountain springs 50 km away. In Syria, huge waterwheels lifted water from the River Orontes to supply crops in the fields. Some of these medieval wheels still survive.

Today, there are many more people living in the Middle East and an even greater demand for water. In the Gulf States, fresh water is made from seawater processed in desalination plants (the salt is taken out). Israel imports water from Turkey by ship, but this supplies only five per cent of the country's needs.

Water is so precious that it can be the cause of disputes. One-third of Israel's fresh water comes from Lake Kinneret. The source of that water is the Golan Heights, which Israel captured from Syria in the Six Day War of 1967. The area remains disputed between the two countries.

Wealth from oil

Many Middle Eastern countries have valuable oil reserves – Saudi Arabia, Iran, Iraq, Oman, Yemen, and the tiny Gulf States of Kuwait, Qatar, Bahrain and the United Arab Emirates. Wealth from oil has allowed these nations to improve their cities, and funded new hospitals and banks.

Old Arab traditions have been strengthened by this new money. Modern buildings have been designed in Islamic style, with arches, domes and decorative tiles. Traditional Arab music is supported by wealthy sponsors, and by the new radio and television stations.

Fearing that one day their oil will run out, many countries have invested in new projects. Bahrain, for example, processes aluminium and manufactures machinery and electrical goods.

Oil refinery

This oil refinery in Kuwait is one of many in the Persian Gulf. Huge tankers pick up oil from coastal terminals, making the Gulf one of the world's busiest seaways.

An unstable region

Many Middle Eastern countries are ruled by royal families, with kings, sultans or emirs at the head. The rich are fabulously rich while the poor live well below the poverty line. Islam plays a strong role in government, but Muslim fundamentalists want even stricter Islamic laws and, despite its great wealth, the Middle East is a tense and unstable region.

Desert golf course
In the wealthy United Arab Emirates, money from oil has been used to create this golf course in the desert.

Traditional dress
In the Gulf States, the traditional dress for men is a dishdasha (a flowing cotton gown). They also wear a headdress to keep off the heat.

CENTRAL ASIA

In 1991, the old Soviet Union broke up. A group of countries in the middle of the Asian continent broke away from Russia and became independent nations for the first time in modern history. They cover a vast region and all kinds of landscapes and climates, from the desert of Turkmenistan to the grasslands of Kazakhstan and the mountains of Kyrgyzstan.

The steppes

Kazakhstan is five times larger than France and almost the size of India. Much of its landscape is covered in grasslands – the steppes. Nomadic herders roam across the steppes on horseback, with their herds of cattle and flocks of sheep. They live in yurts (round felt tents). The Kazakh traditional food is koumiss, a drink made from fermented mare's milk.

In modern times it has become increasingly hard for the Kazakh herders to make a living from raising livestock. Many have been forced to settle on arable farms, or move to the cities to find work in the factories.

The Silk Road

The central Asian nations lie on the ancient trade route between Asia and Europe known as the Silk Road. The cities of Tashkent, Samarkand and Kiva in Uzbekistan were trading centres along this route. These cities are still full of merchants and traders. Bazaars and stalls sell fruit, spices, silk and cotton.

The Silk Road carried not only goods, but also ideas and cultures. A mix of nationalities developed, each with its own identity and language. The people of Kazakhstan, for example, are descendants of Turk and Mongol settlers and speak Kazakh.

Riding skills
The children of Kazakh herders learn to ride at a very early age and spend much of their lives on horseback.

Religious differences

Islam was brought to central Asia in the 7th century and is the main religion today. However, to the west of the Caspian Sea, there is mix of religious faiths. The people of Azerbaijan are mostly Muslims, but in neighbouring Armenia, Christianity is the dominant religion. This mix has been the cause of political tension.

In the early 1990s, a bitter civil war broke out between Armenia and Azerbaijan over Nagorno-Karabakh. This region lies within the borders of Muslim Azerbaijan, but most of its population is Christian and Armenian. A ceasefire was declared in 1994, but the dispute has left 20 per cent of Azerbaijan under Armenian control.

Georgia is a mountainous country where four-fifths of the people are Christians. There is an ongoing armed struggle with the Muslim population of Abkhazia, in the west of the country. They want independence from Georgia.

Everyday life

Most people in the central Asian republics live in modest homes in the villages and towns and struggle to make a living. The cities are developing fast, however, as traders and industrialists from all over the world seek new business opportunities. But many skilled Russians have moved back to Russia. Standards of healthcare, schooling and housing have worsened as a result.

Farming and industry

In mountainous Uzbekistan, Tajikistan and Kyrgyzstan, farmers cultivate the river valleys. In the fertile Fergana Valley of Uzbekistan they grow fruit, rice and cotton.

They also breed silkworms for their cocoons, which are used to make silk. In the sheltered valleys in Georgia, farmers grow grapes to make wine.

Large-scale commercial farming was introduced in the Soviet era. The Russians created elaborate irrigation systems, notably in Turkmenistan, where farms take water from the Karakum Canal, which runs through the south of the country. The rivers flowing into the Aral Sea were used as a water source for the cotton fields in Uzbekistan, Kazakhstan and Turkmenistan. The sea has now shrunk to half of its original size and is surrounded by infertile, salt-laden soil.

Fishing is important for those countries bordering the sea. The Caspian Sea is the

world's main source of caviar – the eggs of the sturgeon fish. Caviar is considered a gourmet food and is very expensive to buy – a 100 g tin can cost more than £100.

During the Soviet era, the Russians also developed mines and set up industries in the region. Factories produce processed foods, textiles, clothing, machinery and chemicals. But the most valuable products of all are oil and natural gas, found beneath the Caspian Sea off Kazakhstan, Turkmenistan and in Azerbaijan. Baku, the capital of Azerbaijan, is now a major centre of the oil industry.

Tourism is also developing in central Asia. The Tian Shan Mountains and the route of the Silk Road are popular attractions. But political unrest in the region deters many visitors.

Shrinking sea

The Aral Sea was once a major lake supplying fish and water to the people living around its shores, but it has shrunk to half its original size.

Cotton pickers

The annual cotton crop of Uzbekistan matches that of the USA. Cotton is known as 'white gold' in the region.

INDIA

With around a billion people, India has the second largest population in the world, but the people only live in about a third of the land space. This results in the cities being overcrowded – trains and buses are often so packed with people that some passengers cling to the roof!

Staple food

Rice is one of the staple foods in India. Rice fields, called paddies, are flooded at the start of the growing season. The seedlings are then planted by hand.

People and worship

Within this large population there are many different languages spoken – Hindu and English are the official languages, with another 14 major languages spoken throughout the country. There are also 845 dialects – out of a world total of 3,950.

Most Indians are followers of Hinduism, an ancient religion with hundreds of gods and heroes, but India is the birthplace of several other religions as well. Buddhism began about 2,500 years ago, when Siddhartha Gautama, who became known as the Buddha, left his wealthy family home and set out on his quest for truth. His teachings, which overturned many Hindu beliefs, spread across India.

Sikhism developed in the Punjab in about AD 1500 and combines many of the beliefs of Hinduism and Islam. Islam itself was introduced to India from the 4th century AD. There are many other religions with smaller numbers of followers, for example Jainism or Zoroastrianism.

Sacred river

Hindus believe that certain rivers can wash away sins. The Ganges is particularly sacred, and many people bathe in its waters.

A variety of spices

Indian cooking is famous all over the world. Complex flavours, spices and the use of fiery-hot chillies are just some of its characteristics. Dishes of rice or bread with dal (puréed beans), mildly spiced vegetables and perhaps small quantities of meat or fish are served at mealtimes.

Food varies greatly from place to place. In southern India, there are rice cakes and stews flavoured with banana. On the west coast, around Goa, meat is cooked with coconut milk. Tandoori food, baked in a clay oven, is very popular in the north-west.

Rice fields and tea leaves

The different climates and landscapes of India influence the type of food produced. Most of the rice is grown in the wetter, tropical climate of the coastal regions, and grain comes from the plains of northern India, especially round the River Ganges.

Darjeeling, in the foothills of the Himalaya Mountain, and the fertile land of the north-eastern state of Assam provide the perfect conditions to grow tea.

India is the largest tea exporter in the world. Tea bushes are grown in huge plantations, and the leaves are plucked by hand and placed in huge baskets carried on the tea-pickers' backs.

Most of India is hot, and every year from June to September, a rainy season sweeps in on the monsoon winds, producing hot and sticky weather. But this rarely touches the Thar Desert, which fills much of the north-west region bordering Pakistan. Millet, sorghum and maize are grown on the edges of the desert, but the driest regions are home only to nomadic camel herders.

Two-thirds of the Indian population live in small villages, making a living through farming. Many are employed by the large plantations, while others farm their own small plots of land.

Little princess
Sikhism is the religion of many people in the state of Punjab, in northern India. Sikh girls take the last name 'Kaur' (princess). Sikh boys are known as 'Singh' (lion).

The caste system

Hinduism is not just a religion, it is a way of life. Hindu society was once divided into castes. At the top were the Brahmans, who were doctors, lawyers, teachers and other professionals. Next came the Kshatriyas, the landowners and large-scale farmers. The third caste were the Vaisyas, the traders. The fourth were the Sudras, ordinary workers. Some people doing menial jobs, such as sweeping the streets and collecting the rubbish, used to be outside the caste system. They lived apart from the rest of society and were known as 'Untouchables'. Today, children are taught that the caste system is not

Painted elephant

Ganesh, the god of prosperity, is portrayed as a man with an elephant's head. To represent Ganesh, real elephants are sometimes painted to take part in religious parades.

Street performers

Jugglers, musicians, snake charmers and acrobats play to enthusiastic audiences in streets and marketplaces all over India.

acceptable. It is not as strong as it used to be, but it still affects what jobs people do, who they marry, what they wear and even what they eat.

Gods and festivals

The stories of Hindu gods are told in famous poems that are sung on special occasions. Brahma is the lord of all creation. Vishnu is the god who preserves life, and he is reborn on earth from time to time to fight evil and to protect mankind. Shiva represents all the forces of nature. The elephant-headed god Ganesh is thought to bring good luck and prosperity. His face can be seen on posters and calendars throughout India.

Hindu festivals are very colourful occasions. Statues of the gods are dressed up and decorated with gold. At the festival of Holi, people run around the streets throwing powdered dye at each other. The dye symbolizes fertility. During Diwali, the festival of lights, lamps are lit in the doors and windows of every house and twinkle like thousands of little stars.

The most spectacular festival is the Kumbha Mela, held every 12 years at Allahabad, where two sacred rivers, the Yamuna and the Ganges, merge. It is the world's largest festival, attended by 12 million people. Five days of celebrations begin with the procession of the sadhus (holy men who have given up all their possessions and live by begging).

Sport and entertainment

Cricket is the country's most popular sport, and children often play it in the streets. When the Indian cricket team plays a test match against England, Australia or Pakistan, millions tune in their radios to listen.

Watching plays is another popular pastime. Travelling theatres take plays based on topical events in the news around the country. In southern India, the Kathakali performers retell stories from the Hindu sacred books wearing vivid make-up and elaborate costumes. Shadow puppets are another traditional entertainment. They tell old stories using mime and sound.

Cricket hero
Saurav Ganguly was born in Calcutta in 1972. He started playing for India when he was still a teenager and later went on to captain the national team. He is considered to be one of India's greatest batsmen.

Bollywood

Mumbai (Bombay) is the centre of India's huge film industry, and it is known around the world by its nickname, 'Bollywood'. More films are produced here than anywhere else in the world, including Hollywood in the USA.

Most Indian films are musical romances, with choreographed fight scenes, spectacular song-and-dance routines and larger-than-life villains and heroes.

The music is played on traditional instruments, such as the stringed sitar, which looks like a long-necked guitar, and the tabla drums. The tabla is a pair of drums consisting of a small wooden, right-hand drum and a larger metal, left-hand drum.

Bollywood films are extremely popular throughout the Indian subcontinent and the actors who star in them can become very rich and famous.

Film stars

Bollywood actors such as Tina Minum, shown here, are huge stars in India.

India today

After 200 years of British rule, India won its independence in 1947. Its democratic, multi-party government is based on the British system.

Two-thirds of the population live in villages, scraping a living by farming. Others work in factories in huge cities such as Delhi and Kolkata (Calcutta), making clothing, chemicals, machinery or electrical equipment. India also has a growing computer industry.

Although some have become wealthy through business, the computer industry or films, the majority of people are poor, doing menial jobs with long hours and low pay. Children as young as five work on farms and in workshops. Their wages are essential to help feed the family.

PAKISTAN

In 1947, when India became independent from Britain, Muslims wanted their own nation separate from the Hindus. British India was divided, with parts of the north becoming Pakistan. At first, Pakistan had two parts, East and West. But in 1971, after a civil war, East Pakistan broke free and became Bangladesh.

Ancient and modern

The Indus river and its tributaries flow through the dry Indus plain that extends across most of Pakistan. Thanks to their waters, one of the world's first civilizations grew up in the Indus Valley 5,000 years ago. Today, the rivers provide water to irrigate the land in the province of Punjab, which is the main agricultural area. Wheat, sugar cane, vegetables and fruit are produced. Rice, grown in flooded paddy fields, is a major export crop. Cotton is also grown here and is used in the textile industry.

Pakistan is a mix of old and new. In cities, such as Islamabad (the capital), there are high-rise buildings and shopping malls.

Apricot harvest

Women from the Hunza region of Pakistan sort freshly picked apricots and arrange them on circular mats to dry in the sun.

In the bazaars, videos, pocket calculators and Japanese watches are sold alongside fruit and vegetables, handmade rugs and carpets. Music cassettes and CDs blare out modern versions of traditional music.

Pakistan is a Muslim country and most women observe the Islamic rule of dressing modestly by wearing a veil to cover their head. Families are large, with an average of seven people in every household. Marriages are traditionally arranged by the family, although young Pakistanis are increasingly finding their own marriage partner.

Political troubles

Since the partition with India, Pakistan has been in dispute with its neighbour over Kashmir, a region in the far north. In 1947, the Hindu leader of Kashmir chose to join India rather than Pakistan, although most of the Kashmiri people are Muslim. The disputed territory remains under Indian control, but it is still a bone of contention leading to violence.

In 1971, East Pakistan demanded independence. After months of civil war, it declared itself a new nation, Bangladesh.

Pakistan was again thrown into crisis in September 2001, when the US-led attacks on neighbouring Afghanistan threatened to upset Pakistan's stability. There were mass demonstrations against the US attacks, but Pakistan's military government restrained the demonstrators and gave support to the USA.

Language

There are several ethnic groups in Pakistan. The remote mountains in the north of the country are home to the Gujars, who live as nomadic herders. Many people who live on the border with Afghanistan are Pashtuns, who have a reputation as warriors. The people of the Punjab region are mainly farmers. Urdu is the official language in Pakistan, but the different ethnic groups also have their own languages – Pushtu, Punjabi, Sindhi, Saraiki and Baluchi are spoken in different parts of the region.

Education

More than 40 per cent of the population is under the age of 15. Education is free, but it is not compulsory. Only one-third of the children of primary school age go to school. Even so, classes are large, with more than 40 pupils to every teacher. This lack of schooling means that only 54 per cent of men and 24 per cent of women can read and write.

School children

These schoolgirls in Karachi are learning to read and write. Even though schooling is free, some families choose not to educate their daughters.

THE REST OF SOUTHERN ASIA

The landmass made up of India and the neighbouring countries is often called the Indian subcontinent. The north is hemmed in by the Himalaya Mountains and the south is surrounded by the tropical Indian Ocean. To the west is the high land of Afghanistan, and to the east is low-lying Bangladesh.

Nepal

Nepal lies in the Himalaya Mountains. In the north of the country, at 4,200 m above sea level, the people live by farming, growing grain and vegetables, and herding sheep and goats. They also keep yaks (long-haired cattle that can only live at this height). Yaks are used to carry goods along the

Buddhist temple

The eyes of the Buddha are painted on the four faces of the Bodnath Stupa in Nepal. Stupas are ancient burial mounds believed to contain relics of early holy men. Prayer flags flutter from lines attached to the stupa, scattering prayers into the wind.

mountain paths. They also provide milk, meat and leather. The southern part of the country, which is not so mountainous, is the main agricultural region. Here, the fertile soil produces rice and maize, vegetables and fruit.

Most of the people are very poor and live in mud brick or wooden houses. The capital, Kathmandu, which lies in the middle of Nepal at a height of 1,340 m above sea level, is the only city in a country of 22 million people.

Most people are Hindus, and some believe that the king is the reincarnation of the god Vishnu. Until 1990, monarchs had absolute power in the country. But nationwide unrest forced the king to accept a parliamentary system. In 2001, the crown prince assassinated his father and other members of the royal family and then shot himself. The king's brother took over, but the royal family's authority has been damaged.

Tourism is a valuable source of income. Visitors come on trekking expeditions, or to climb in the Himalayas. Mount Everest (8,848 m) is the world's highest mountain. Local Sherpa people provide assistance as guides and porters.

Bhutan shepherdess

This young Bhutan girl is wearing the traditional kiri dress. Like most of the population, her family makes a living by farming.

Bhutan

To the east of Nepal, also bordering China, lies the tiny mountain kingdom of Bhutan. This is a devout Buddhist country, with 1,300 monasteries. Until 1998, the king ruled over the population of two million people with absolute power, preserving their traditional society by restricting visitors and banning Western influences, such as television. The monarch, known as Druk Gyalpo (dragon king), now shares power with a government.

National dress is compulsory. Men wear a gho (a knee-length wrap-around), and women wear a kira (an ankle-length dress). People live by herding yaks, or by growing potatoes, wheat and rice in the lowlands.

Jute harvest

Jute is grown in the wetlands of Bangladesh. The long, fibrous stems are used to make sacking and mats.

Delta country

To the south of Bhutan the land flattens out into the low plain occupied by Bangladesh. Two great rivers, the Brahmaputra and the Ganges, flow south from the Himalayas and cross the plain. Joined by the River Meghna in the east, they form numerous channels and create a huge delta that runs into the Bay of Bengal. This well-watered land is good for growing crops, but the rivers often burst their banks when the Himalayan snow melts in the spring and summer, causing floods. Worse still, the region is often hit by devastating storms called cyclones. These cause tidal waves that surge up the rivers and wash whole villages away. Many people have been killed by such disasters. In 1970, half a million people died beneath a 15 m tidal wave. Bangladesh struggles to feed its population of 126 million people because of these natural disasters.

Three-quarters of the population live by farming, growing rice and vegetables. The most important export, however, is clothing. Foreign companies come to Bangladesh because the people work for low wages, which keeps the cost of the finished clothes down. More recently, factories have produced hi-tech television and computer components.

Millions of children work on farms and in factories, but the Bangladesh government and charities are doing much to end child labour and improve primary education.

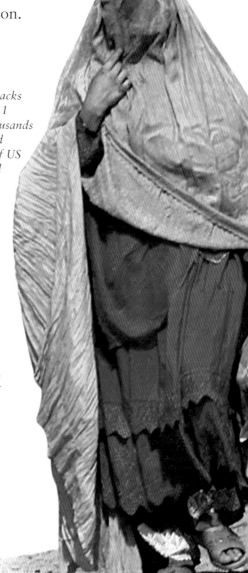

Refugees

After the terrorist attacks against the USA on 11 September 2001, thousands of Afghan people fled their homes in fear of US attacks. They crossed the borders to Pakistan and Iran and stayed in refugee camps.

Traffic jam

There are more than 300,000 rickshaws in Dhaka, the capital of Bangladesh. They provide a taxi service for the city's 12.3 million people. Most of these brightly coloured vehicles are driven by pedal power.

War-torn Afghanistan

Afghanistan is inhabited by a number of mainly Muslim peoples who live by traditional farming, growing grains, fruits and nuts in the river valleys, and herding sheep in the sparse mountain pastures. It was a monarchy until 1973, when the army overthrew the king. This was the beginning of decades of unrest.

In 1979, the Soviet Union invaded to prop up a pro-communist regime that had seized power in a coup. For ten years it tried to conquer the country, fighting a vicious war against Islamic resistance fighters, the mujaheddin (holy warriors). When the Soviet army finally withdrew, the Afghan people fought among themselves for control of the country. This civil war was brought to an end in the 1990s by the Taliban, who took control of almost all the country, and introduced a very strict kind of Islamic law and code of behaviour.

All music, films and videos were banned. Women could not work for pay, or be seen in public, except when covered from head to foot in the burka (a traditional robe). Children could not do anything that might distract them from religious studies, such as fly kites or play chess. Girls could not go to school.

The Taliban allowed a terrorist group called Al-Qa'ida, led by Osama bin Laden, to build training camps in Afghanistan. Al-Qa'ida were suspected of destroying the World Trade Center in New York City on 11 September 2001. When the Taliban refused to hand over Osama bin Laden, a US-led coalition launched war on the Taliban in Afghanistan. Shortly after the USA began a bombing campaign, the anti-Taliban Northern Alliance captured the capital Kabul and most of the country, and the Taliban were removed from power. A new coalition government was formed.

Tea pickers

The hills in the centre of Sri Lanka are covered with tea bushes. Women pick the tea, selecting only the delicate young shoots. These are rolled, dried and heated, then packed in wooden chests for export.

Stilt fishermen

Villagers on the south-west coast of Sri Lanka perch on poles to do their fishing. Nobody knows how or why this strange technique originated, but stilts in good positions are much prized and are passed on from father to son.

Sri Lanka

Sri Lanka is a tropical island off the south-east coast of India. From the palm-fringed beaches that line the coast, the land rises to high hills that provide the perfect conditions for growing tea. The islanders also grow rubber trees, from which rubber is extracted, and cinnamon trees, the bark of which is peeled off to use as a cooking spice. Much of the south-west of the island is covered with rainforest, where timber is collected with the help of elephants. There are, however, conservation concerns about the destruction of the rainforest.

Precious and semi-precious stones, such as sapphires, rubies, topaz and moonstones are mined in Sri Lanka. The country also has hundreds of workshops where clothes are made for export.

Early settlers in Sri Lanka were the Sinhalese, who came here from India in about 400 BC. In the 11th century, a second wave of immigrants arrived, the darker-skinned Tamils from southern India. The British ruled Sri Lanka from 1796. After independence in

1948, the Sinhalese, who are mainly Buddhist, took control. This caused resentment among the Tamils, who are mainly Hindu. In the 1980s, a guerrilla army called the Tamil Tigers started a war of terrorism against the Sinhalese. The conflict continues today, effectively dividing the island in two. It has badly affected the blossoming tourist trade.

The Maldives

The Maldives is a set of coral islands lying 640 km to the south-west of Sri Lanka. Only 200 of the 1,200 islands are inhabited. Many are just tiny discs of white sand, with clusters of coconut palms growing in the shallow soil.

None of the islands is more than 2.4 m above sea level, making the Maldives the world's flattest country. For this reason, the local people are very concerned about rising sea levels. Some scientists have calculated that as a result of global warming, the sea may rise by as much as one metre by the year 2100. This would flood most of the islands.

Pineapples, pomegranates, bananas, yams and breadfruit (a huge tree fruit that is cooked like a vegetable) grow on the islands. The Maldivians are good sailors and they have a valuable fishing industry. Large catches of tuna and bonito are sold to Japan.

Increasing numbers of people make a living from the tourist trade. Many of the islands now have small luxury hotels on them. Guests arrive by boat and stay in beach houses.

Paradise island

The Maldives is an increasingly popular holiday destination. Tourists spend the days relaxing on the beaches, or diving and snorkelling among the spectacular coral reefs.

 **AFGHANISTAN**

Capital
Kabul
Area
652,225 km²
Population
18,800,000
Population density
29 per km²
Life expectancy
43 (m); 44 (f)
Religion
Islam
Languages
Pashto, Dari (dialect of Farsi or Iranian) and many local languages
Adult literacy rate
31 per cent
Currency
afghani

 **ARMENIA**

Capital
Yerevan
Area
29,800 km²
Population
3,795,000
Population density
119 per km²
Life expectancy
67 (m); 74 (f)
Religion
Christianity
Languages
Armenian, Kurdish
Adult literacy rate
99 per cent
Currency
dram

AZERBAIJAN

Capital
Baku
Area
86,600 km²
Population
7,983,000
Population density
88 per km²
Life expectancy
65 (m); 74 (f)
Religions
Islam, Christianity
Language
Azerbaijani (Azeri)
Adult literacy rate
97 per cent
Currency
manat

 BAHRAIN

Capital
Al Manamah
Area
695 km²
Population
666,000
Population density
921 per km²
Life expectancy
66 (m); 69 (f)
Religion
Islam
Languages
Arabic, English
Adult literacy rate
85 per cent
Currency
Bahraini dinar

 BANGLADESH

Capital
Dhaka
Area
147,570 km²
Population
126,947,000
Population density
845 per km²
Life expectancy
57 (m); 56 (f)
Religions
Islam, Hinduism
Language
Bengali
Adult literacy rate
38 per cent
Currency
taka

 BHUTAN

Capital
Thimphu
Area
46,500 km²
Population
692,000
Population density
43 per km²
Life expectancy
49 (m); 52 (f)
Religions
Buddhism, Hinduism
Languages
Dzongkha (Tibetan dialect), Nepali and other local languages
Adult literacy rate
42 per cent
Currency
ngultrum

 **CYPRUS**

Capital
Nicosia
Area
9,251 km²
Population
753,000
Population density
81 per km²
Life expectancy
75 (m); 79 (f)
Religions
Christianity, Islam
Languages
Greek, Turkish
Adult literacy rate
94 per cent
Currency
Cyprus pound

 **GEORGIA**

Capital
Tbilisi
Area
69,700 km²
Population
5,399,000
Population density
73 per km²
Life expectancy
68 (m); 76 (f)
Religions
Christianity, Islam
Language
Georgian
Adult literacy rate
99 per cent
Currency
lari

 **INDIA**

Capital
New Delhi
Area
3,287,263 km²
Population
1,030,000,000
Population density
295 per km²
Life expectancy
57 (m); 58 (f)
Religions
Hinduism, Islam, Christianity,
Sikhism
Languages
Hindi, English, and local
languages
Adult literacy rate
52 per cent
Currency
rupee

 **IRAN**

Capital
Tehran
Area
1,648,000 km²
Population
62,746,000
Population density
38 per km²
Life expectancy
58 (m); 59 (f)
Religion
Islam
Languages
Farsi (Iranian), Turkic and
other local languages
Adult literacy rate
72 per cent
Currency
Iranian rial

 **IRAQ**

Capital
Baghdad
Area
438,317 km²
Population
22,450,000
Population density
50 per km²
Life expectancy
77 (m); 78 (f)
Religion
Islam
Language
Arabic
Adult literacy rate
58 per cent
Currency
Iraqi dinar

 **ISRAEL**

Capital
Jerusalem
Area
21,946 km²
Population
6,125,000
Population density
272 per km²
Life expectancy
75 (m); 79 (f)
Religions
Judaism, Islam, Christianity
Languages
Hebrew, Russian, Arabic,
European languages
Adult literacy rate
96 per cent
Currency
new shekel

 **JORDAN**

Capital
Amman
Area
97,740 km²
Population
5,132,000
Population density
64 per km²
Life expectancy
66 (m); 69 (f)
Religion
Islam
Language
Arabic
Adult literacy rate
87 per cent
Currency
dinar

 KAZAKHSTAN

Capital
Astana
Area
2,717,300 km²
Population
14,942,000
Population density
6 per km²
Life expectancy
64 (m); 73 (f)
Religion
Islam
Languages
Kazakh, Russian
Adult literacy rate
97 per cent
Currency
tenge

 **KUWAIT**

Capital
Kuwait City
Area
17,818 km²
Population
2,107,000
Population density
114 per km²
Life expectancy
71 (m); 73 (f)
Religion
Islam
Languages
Arabic, English
Adult literacy rate
79 per cent
Currency
Kuwaiti dinar

 KYRGYZSTAN

Capital
Bishkek
Area
198,500 km²
Population
4,823,000
Population density
24 per km²
Life expectancy
61 (m); 70 (f)
Religion
Islam
Languages
Kyrgyz (Cyrillic script; Latin script to be reintroduced), Russian
Adult literacy rate
98 per cent
Currency
som

 LEBANON

Capital
Beirut
Area
10,452 km²
Population
3,236,000
Population density
305 per km²
Life expectancy
66 (m); 70 (f)
Religions
Islam, Christianity
Languages
Arabic, French, Kurdish, Armenian
Adult literacy rate
92 per cent
Currency
Lebanese pound

 MALDIVES

Capital
Malé
Area
298 km²
Population
278,000
Population density
916 per km²
Life expectancy
67 (m); 67 (f)
Religion
Islam
Language
Divehi (Maldivian, related to Sinhala)
Adult literacy rate
93 per cent
Currency
rufiyaa

NEPAL

Capital
Kathmandu
Area
147,181 km²
Population
22,367
Population density
148 per km²
Life expectancy
48 (m); 50 (f)
Religions
Hinduism, Buddhism
Languages
Nepali, Maithir, Bhojpuri
Adult literacy rate
27 per cent
Currency
Nepalese rupee

 **OMAN**

Capital
Muscat
Area
309,500 km²
Population
2,460,000
Population density
7 per km²
Life expectancy
67 (m); 71 (f)
Religion
Islam
Languages
Arabic, English
Adult literacy rate
41 per cent
Currency
Omani rial

 **PAKISTAN**

Capital
Islamabad
Area
796,095 km²
Population
134,510,000
Population density
164 per km²
Life expectancy
59 (m); 59 (f)
Religion
Islam
Languages
Urdu, Punjabi, Pushto, Sindhi,
Saraiki, English
Adult literacy rate
38 per cent
Currency
Pakistani rupee

 QATAR

Capital
Doha
Area
11,437 km²
Population
589,000
Population density
47 per km²
Life expectancy
68 (m); 74 (f)
Religion
Islam
Languages
Arabic, English
Adult literacy rate
79 per cent
Currency
Qatari riyal

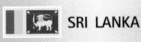 **SAUDI ARABIA**

Capital
Riyadh
Area
2,240,000 km²
Population
19,895,000
Population density
9 per km²
Life expectancy
68 (m); 71 (f)
Religion
Islam
Language
Arabic
Adult literacy rate
63 per cent
Currency
riyal

 SRI LANKA

Capital
Colombo
Area
65,610 km²
Population
19,043,000
Population density
286 per km²
Life expectancy
67 (m); 71 (f)
Religions
Buddhism, Hinduism,
Christianity, Islam
Languages
Sinhala, Tamil, English
Adult literacy rate
90 per cent
Currency
Sri Lanka rupee

SYRIA

Capital
Damascus
Area
185,180 km²
Population
16,110,000
Population density
87 per km²
Life expectancy
64 (m); 68 (f)
Religion
Islam
Languages
Arabic, Kurdish
Adult literacy rate
79 per cent
Currency
Syrian pound

 TAJIKISTAN

Capital
Dushanbe
Area
143,100 km²
Population
6,237,000
Population density
43 per km²
Life expectancy
65 (m); 71 (f)
Religion
Islam
Languages
Tajik (Cyrillic script), Russian
Adult literacy rate
98 per cent
Currency
somoni

 **TURKEY**

Capital
Ankara
Area
774,815 km²
Population
64,385,000
Population density
83 per km²
Life expectancy
68 (m); 73 (f)
Religion
Islam
Languages
Turkish, Kurdish and others
Adult literacy rate
82 per cent
Currency
Turkish lira

TURKMENISTAN

Capital
Ashgabat
Area
488,100 km²
Population
4,384,000
Population density
10 per km²
Life expectancy
62 (m); 68 (f)
Religion
Islam
Language
Turkmen (Latin-based script)
Adult literacy rate
98 per cent
Currency
manat

UNITED ARAB EMIRATES

Capital
Abu Dhabi
Area
77,700 km²
Population
2,938,000
Population density
35 per km²
Life expectancy
72 (m); 75 (f)
Religion
Islam
Languages
Arabic, English
Adult literacy rate
79 per cent
Currency
dirham

UZBEKISTAN

Capital
Tashkent
Area
447,400 km²
Population
23,954,000
Population density
54 per km²
Life expectancy
66 (m); 72 (f)
Religion
Islam
Languages
Uzbek, Russian, Kazakh
Adult literacy rate
97 per cent
Currency
som

YEMEN

Capital
San'a
Area
527,968 km²
Population
17,676,000
Population density
32 per km²
Life expectancy
55 (m); 56 (f)
Religion
Islam
Language
Arabic
Adult literacy rate
38 per cent
Currency
Yemeni riyal

Eastern Asia
MONGOLIA

Great rolling grasslands dominate the landscape of Mongolia, a vast country that lies between Russia and China. The Altai Mountains tower in the west, and the Gobi Desert covers much of the south. Despite its size, Mongolia has a population of just 2.6 million. On average, there are fewer than two people per km².

Mongolia is one of the highest countries in the world – on average it is 1,580 m above sea level. Its highest mountains are in the far west. The Altai Mountains are permanently snowcapped, but between the peaks are stark deserts where rain hardly ever falls. Although landlocked, the country has many lakes for water supplies and fishing. The south is dominated by the Gobi Desert. It looks barren, but it has enough grass to support scattered herds of goats and camels. Much of the rest of Mongolia is grassland.

Practical clothing

A deel (long cloth gown) forms the basis of Mongolian clothing. Its long sleeves can be rolled down to keep the hands warm.

Nomadic life

Traditionally, most Mongolian families lived as semi-nomadic herders, moving around the steppes with their herds of cattle, sheep, horses and camels. The herders moved at least twice a year, seeking new pasture for their animals. They lived in gers (large round tents). Made of felt material supported on wooden slats, gers could be quickly put up and taken down. They were surprisingly spacious and comfortable, with room for beds and furniture. All gers had a similar layout. The door always faced south, there was a place of honour set aside for guests, and treasured possessions were kept at the back of the ger. On the back wall was the family altar, with Buddhist images and family photos. Besides their main ger, Mongolian people also erected smaller gers for storage purposes.

Today, however, most rural people live on large livestock farms. Few follow the nomadic way of life.

Mobile television

A nomadic family gathers outside their ger (dwelling) in the Mongolian steppes to watch a mobile television, powered by an electricity generator.

On the road

Most Mongolian roads are little more than dirt tracks. They are dusty in the hot summers, muddy after heavy rains, and frozen hard during the long, cold winters. Herders use two-humped Bactrian camels to carry their possessions from place to place. Horses are also very important to Mongolian nomads – but not just for transport. Airak, the nation's most popular drink, is made from mare's milk that has been fermented for about three days to make it slightly fizzy. Mongolians live mainly on a diet of milk, cheese and meat. They do not eat many vegetables because so little of the land is suitable for growing crops.

Festivals and culture

Children of herding families are taught at home until the age of eight, when they are sent to small boarding schools in the towns or in the capital, Ulan Bator. All Mongolians learn to ride at a young age. In the summer children take part in horse-racing festivals, such as the great Naadam festival in Ulan Bator. It also includes other popular Mongolian sports, such as wrestling and archery.

In the capital, most people live in apartment blocks and work in offices and factories. But they still love rural life, and many keep a ger on the outskirts of the city. Listening to music is a favourite pastime. Mongolians sing traditional songs of love, adventure and life on the steppes, accompanied by a two-stringed morin khour, which is played a bit like a cello.

Young rider

Mongolian children learn to ride horses at a young age and enjoy taking part in horse-racing festivals. This boy is competing in the annual Naadam festival.

CHINA

One person in every five in the world is Chinese. With 1,275 million citizens, the country has the largest population of any nation on earth. China covers a huge area of eastern Asia, but most of the people live in the eastern part of the country, where the river valleys and plains are good for farming, and where most of the big industrial cities are clustered.

Workshop of the world

For many years, the communist Chinese government had control and ownership of all industries and food production. During this time, China virtually cut itself off from the outside world.

Since the 1980s, the government has given greater freedom to people to develop businesses for themselves and encouraged more international trade. Now China is booming. Cities of high-rise office blocks are being built, drawing in millions of workers from the countryside. Shenzen, for example, was a small market town just 20 years ago, and now it has a population of over three million. The economic development of the past 20 years is mostly concentrated in Special Economic Zones in eastern China where foreigners have set up joint enterprises with the Chinese. Factories in these areas now produce a full range of goods from clothes to computer chips.

New ways

China has become less cut off from the rest of the world, and most cities now have fast-food restaurants selling American-style burgers.

Boom town

Shenzen has grown rapidly in recent years. Its economic boom is mainly thanks to its location. It is near to Hong Kong, an old British colony and a world financial centre.

Old ways, new world

Traditional ways of life survive alongside modern developments, even in the big cities, such as Shanghai, Guangzhou (Canton) and Hong Kong. Pedal-power tri-shaw taxis gather in the squares, waiting for customers, and the street markets are packed with spices, fish and fresh vegetables. Stalls sell snacks – dishes of rice and noodles eaten with chopsticks – freshly cooked in woks.

Chinese herbal medicines and the ancient art of acupuncture (inserting sharp needles into specific parts of the body) are used alongside Western medicine. Many keep fit by practising old martial arts such as t'ai chi ch'uan in the public squares.

Ping-pong is still one of China's most popular sports. Traditional entertainments such as the circus, with its spectacularly skilled acrobats, and the opera, with its colourful tales of myth and legend retold through songs and dance, are always well attended. The Chinese New Year is celebrated with feasts, firecrackers and displays by dancing dragon puppets.

Communist control

The dramatic economic changes in China have not been matched by political reform. The government still remains a one-party communist state, exerting control over many aspects of people's lives. The media is not allowed to criticise the government and political opponents can be imprisoned. This was made clear to the world in 1989, when the army crushed a peaceful revolt in Tiananmen Square, Beijing, led by students demanding greater freedom and democracy.

Feeding and looking after the huge population is China's most pressing task. For many years the government has attempted to slow population growth by encouraging families to have only one child. All one-child families are rewarded with priority housing and medical care.

Agriculture

Children in farming villages often help their parents in the fields. Many Chinese farmers still use labour-intensive, hand- or ox-powered equipment.

The many faces of China

Despite the rapid growth of cities, two-thirds of China's population still lives in the countryside. Most farming villages have few of the hi-tech gadgets and comforts of the new cities. Simple one-storey homes have just two rooms under a tiled roof. Pigs and chickens live in the muddy pens outside. The fields are often worked by ox-drawn ploughs and hand-held shovels.

Ways of life differ with the climate and landscape. In Manchuria (Dongbei) in the far north-east, the winters are bitterly cold, but the summers are long enough to grow good harvests of wheat, soya beans, sugar beet, sunflowers and cotton. The Manchurian forests produce much of the timber used in China's industry and the area is rich in minerals, notably coal and oil.

In the far west, people live in and around the cities that once stood on the ancient overland trade routes called the Silk Road. They include nomadic Kazakh herders, who live in yurts (felt tents), and Persian-speaking Tajiks.

China is the world's leading producer of rice, most of which is produced in the warm and humid region to the south of the great River Chang Jiang (Yangtze), which runs through the middle of the country.

In the south-west lies Xizang (Tibet). Chinese rule over this Buddhist land, set high in the Himalayas, is a source of conflict. Many Tibetans want independence from China and the return of their spiritual leader, the Dalai Lama, who lives in exile.

Novice monks

Boys as young as eight are sent to Buddhist monasteries in Tibet to train as monks. They are allowed few possessions and spend much of their time meditating.

Food also varies from region to region. Specialities of the south-eastern region include the fried noodle dish châo mien (chow mein), and dim sum (dumplings steamed in bamboo baskets). In Tibet, the main food is tsampa (flat bread made with barley flour) eaten with a soup-like tea flavoured with yak butter.

Ancient wonders

Some 90 per cent of the Chinese people belong to the Han ethnic group, but there are 55 official minority ethnic groups, each with its own customs and language.

Mandarin is the official language of China, but there are many other Chinese languages, such as Wu and Cantonese. The Chinese written language is not based on sounds, but on pictures which have evolved into 'characters'. This means that written Chinese can be read by most Chinese speakers, regardless of the form of Chinese that they speak – they see the same character, understand its meaning, but pronounce it differently.

Calligraphy – the art of writing beautiful Chinese characters using a brush and ink – often forms part of paintings, on sheets of paper or silk.

Street painting

An audience of Chinese school children watches an artist produce a giant-sized painting using a big brush and a bucket of ink.

Extraordinarily delicate and skilled paintings, many hundreds of years old, are evidence of China's history as one of the world's oldest and most sophisticated civilizations. It was ruled over by emperors for more than 2,000 years. Tourists from all over the world come to see the remains of this civilization. The Great Wall of China and the clay army buried with the first emperor at Xi'an in 210 BC are popular attractions. Once the emperors' grand Forbidden City at the heart of Beijing was out of bounds to everyone who was not a noble, but now it is open for all to wonder at and admire.

TAIWAN

L ying 160 km off the coast of south-east China, the large island of Taiwan is a prosperous, industrialized nation. Much of the population come originally from mainland China, having fled communist rule. A high ridge of forest-cloaked mountains lines the eastern coast, but most people live in the broad, fertile plains that stretch out to the west coast.

When communists won control of China in 1949 following a bloody civil war, some two million defeated nationalists fled to Taiwan. They set up an alternative government, claiming to be the true Republic of China, and waited for the opportunity to return to the mainland. This has never happened. China has repeatedly threatened to take over Taiwan, but the Taiwanese have support from the USA.

Taiwan became a fast-growing industrial nation, producing clothes and electrical goods. It also became a leading producer of large-scale industrial products such as petro-chemicals, ships and aircraft as well as hi-tech goods such as computers and silicon chips.

Farms produce rice, sweet potatoes and other vegetables, but often the plains are shrouded in smog from the thousands of factories, especially around Taipei, the capital city, where a third of the population lives.

There are about 200,000 original Taiwanese inhabitants, but 85 per cent of the people came originally from China. They speak Mandarin, eat Chinese food and practise Buddhism. They have also adopted American and Japanese pastimes, such as golf and karaoke.

Dragon boats

Every year a dragon boat festival takes place in Taiwan's capital, Taipei. Competing teams row their dragon-shaped boats to the beat of a drum.

JAPAN

Lying off the east Asia coast, Japan is one of the world's leading industrial nations, famous for producing hi-tech electronic goods. It is governed by a democratically elected parliament, called the Diet, and the head of state is Emperor Akihito. The four main islands are connected by some of the world's biggest, and most technically brilliant, bridges and tunnels.

Industrial power

Japanese society is built on very solid foundations and cultural traditions. They believe strongly in loyalty, and people tend to work for the same employer for the whole of their lives. Many of the world's most familiar product names are Japanese, such as Nissan and Sony.

For many years it seemed that the rise of Japan's wealth was unstoppable, as Japanese companies expanded worldwide. But in the late 1990s, the world economy began to shrink, and Japan's fortunes suddenly began to decline.

Modern city

Much of Japan's capital, Tokyo, was destroyed by bombs in World War II. Today, it is a city of high-rise office blocks and sprawling suburbs.

The spirit world

Most people in Japan believe in a mixture of Shinto and Buddhism. Many festivals revolve around Shinto. They include harvest festivals and the Oshogatsu (New Year) festival, when people go to a shrine to find out their prospects from pieces of paper with their fortunes printed on them.

Girls have their own Shinto festival day, Ohinamatsuri, when parents display dolls in honour of their daughters. For the boys' festival, Tango no Sekku, thousands of streamers shaped like carp are hung in the streets. In November, at Shichi-go-san (seven-five-three), seven-year-old girls, boys of five and girls and boys of three, go to shrines in their finest traditional costumes to be blessed. On special occasions, Japanese girls put on a kimono (a traditional silk robe which is decorated with intricate patterns and pictures).

Shinto, which means 'the way of the gods', is a celebration of life and nature, and involves the worship of the kami (spirits) that are the creative forces in nature. Shrines are dedicated to a specific kami, and are often found in places of spectacular natural beauty. Origami (the art of folding sheets of paper into shapes) is often used to decorate Shinto shrines.

Nature plays an important part in Japanese religion. Every spring, millions go 'cherry-blossom viewing', and the gardens of the Zen Buddhists combine elements such as raked gravel and large rocks.

Festivals

Girls wear traditional, colourful kimonos (robes) when visiting Shinto temples for religious festivals.

Raw fish and seaweed

The Japanese eat dishes of fresh vegetables with meat or seafood. Rice is the main accompaniment. Yakitori (skewers of grilled chicken) is a popular kind of Japanese fast-food, often bought from street vendors. Tempura is deep-fried seafood or vegetables coated in a light batter. Sushi consists of bite-sized rice bundles flavoured with vegetables and wrapped in thin sheets of seaweed, or topped with slices of raw fish.

The Japanese are the world's biggest fish-eaters and their large and modern fishing fleets take ten per cent of the world's catch. Japan produces almost all its own food. This is a remarkable feat, given that less than 20 per cent of the land is suitable for agriculture. Most of Japan is covered by high mountains, and virtually all the cities are on or close to the coast. This includes the capital, Tokyo, which has grown and merged with Yokohama to form the world's largest city, with over 27 million people. But there are still hundreds of old villages in rural areas, with clusters of ancient wooden houses under thatched or tiled roofs.

Fish lunch

These Japanese school children are enjoying a packed lunch of sushi. They eat the fish and rice bundles using chop sticks.

The strength of tradition

The cities are busy with traffic, neon signs, offices, shops, food stalls, discos and bars. Many of the buildings are modern – although they tend to be low rather than high – as Japan suffers regularly from earthquakes. A massive earthquake hit the city of Kobe, on Honshu Island, in 1995, killing more than 5,000 people and injuring 26,000 more. Small, harmless earth tremors are recorded every day.

Old traditions survive among the modern buildings. Houses and apartments have sliding screens made of paper, which separate the rooms. Flat-owners make tiny Zen gardens on their balconies using bonzai (miniature) trees. They may sleep on tatami floor mats. Some larger homes still have a tea-house in the garden, where the 500-year-old cha-no-yu (tea ceremony) can be performed, using carefully chosen pottery to serve whisked and frothy green tea.

Traditional music and theatre are also popular. Gagaku (the ancient court music of Japan) is played by an ensemble of Japanese wind, string and percussion instruments. In noh plays, performers wear masks, and act and dance, while bunraku theatre brings puppets to life.

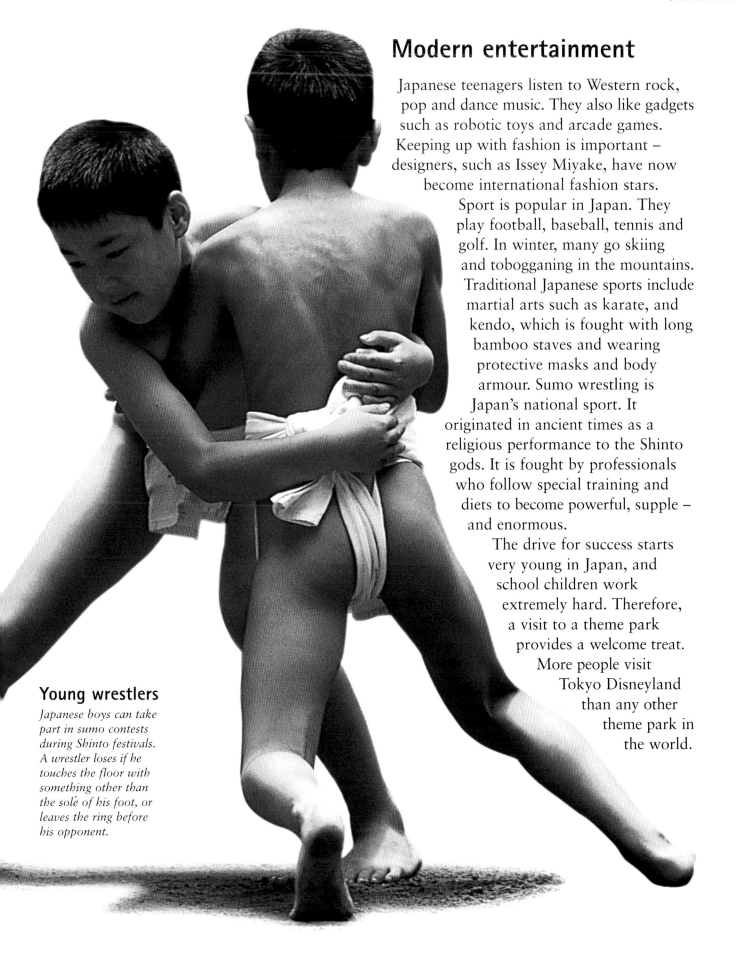

Modern entertainment

Japanese teenagers listen to Western rock, pop and dance music. They also like gadgets such as robotic toys and arcade games. Keeping up with fashion is important – designers, such as Issey Miyake, have now become international fashion stars.

Sport is popular in Japan. They play football, baseball, tennis and golf. In winter, many go skiing and tobogganing in the mountains. Traditional Japanese sports include martial arts such as karate, and kendo, which is fought with long bamboo staves and wearing protective masks and body armour. Sumo wrestling is Japan's national sport. It originated in ancient times as a religious performance to the Shinto gods. It is fought by professionals who follow special training and diets to become powerful, supple – and enormous.

The drive for success starts very young in Japan, and school children work extremely hard. Therefore, a visit to a theme park provides a welcome treat. More people visit Tokyo Disneyland than any other theme park in the world.

Young wrestlers

Japanese boys can take part in sumo contests during Shinto festivals. A wrestler loses if he touches the floor with something other than the sole of his foot, or leaves the ring before his opponent.

KOREA

The broad peninsula of Korea sticks out like a thumb from China towards Japan. The landscape ranges from high mountains and forests to fertile plains. Summers are warm and sunny, but the winters are very cold. In autumn, the leaves of the gingko, poplar and maple trees blaze with yellow, red and gold.

Divided nation

In the early decades of the 20th century, Korea was ruled by Japan. But after the Japanese left at the end of World War II, the country was split in two. In 1948, a communist government under Kim Il Sung took over in North Korea, and, in 1950, North Korea invaded the South. The Korean War (1950–53) pitched the North (supported by China) against the South (supported by the United Nations). At the peace treaty, the peninsula was once again divided in two.

The two halves of Korea are very different. North Korea is communist. The people work on government-owned farms, in the mines producing coal, iron and copper, and in factories. Isolated from the rest of the world, the North Koreans remain poor. In contrast, South Korea has become one of the region's leading industrial nations. Many families were split up by the division of Korea. For years North Korea refused any contact with the South, but it now allows limited exchange visits.

Land of traditions

Korea has a distinctive language, with its own alphabet, called hangul, based entirely on sounds.

Entertainment

Folk songs are popular in both North and South Korea. These North Korean children are playing accordions.

Mountain land

Korea is a mountainous country, but the mountain areas are largely uninhabited.

The peninsula also has its own kinds of food. Bulgogi is sometimes called the 'Korean barbecue'. Strips of meat are cooked at the table on a dome-shaped hot-plate. Shin Sul Ro is a meat stew, with vegetables and nuts, and is popular as a winter warmer. Some Koreans still eat dishes made of dog and snake. But most famous of all is the Korean speciality called kimchi, a kind of pickle that accompanies most meals. In autumn, groups of families and friends gather to make large quantities of winter kimchi. Cabbage and white radish are chopped up, mixed with red chilli peppers, onion, garlic and salt, and then placed in large pottery jars, which are then buried in the garden, or placed on a cool balcony to ferment.

Buddhism and Christianity are the dominant religions in South Korea. There is also a Korean religion called Ch'ondogyo, which combines Christianity, Buddhism, Chinese philosophies and ancient beliefs. Beautiful multi-storied pagoda temples and statues of Buddha are located throughout Korea.

SOUTH-EAST ASIA

The countries of South-east Asia occupy a large chunk of hilly mainland, plus a long, thin peninsula and thousands of islands. There are more than 13,000 islands in Indonesia, and some 7,000 in the Philippines. Plants grow well in the warm climate, watered by frequent rains, and heavy downpours during the rainy season, which lasts almost half the year.

Many of the hilly areas are covered in tropical forest. Elsewhere, step-like terraces have been cut into hillsides to grow rice in flooded fields, quilting the landscape with patches of vivid emerald-green. Mighty rivers, such as the Mekong and Irrawaddy, thread through the larger landmasses, and serve as transport routes for riverboats carrying passengers and goods to towns far inland.

The hot climate has a strong influence on the way people live. The traditional dress in many of these countries is a sarong (a simple, wrap-around skirt). Made of a broad strip of printed cotton cloth, it may be worn by both

Stilt house

This home in northern Vietnam has been built on stilts so that it will not be flooded during the heavy rains of the annual monsoon (rainy) season.

men and women. Houses often have shutters instead of glass windows, as they allow the air to circulate. Village houses are often raised above the ground on stilts, so they are not flooded in very heavy rains.

In Bangkok, the capital of Thailand, an area called the Klongs is permanently flooded by the Chao Phraya river – so all the houses are built on very long stilts. The canals between the houses serve as streets, and the only way to travel about is by boat. Floating shops bring fresh vegetables and household goods.

Headmen and presidents

For most people in South-east Asia, the village is the most important centre of activity. Even large cities in Indonesia and Malaysia have kampongs (village-like areas). Traditionally, the villages are made up of family groups or clans, ruled by a headman and his council. Village leaders will try to get everyone to

agree before any vital decision is made, a process known as 'consensus'. The national governments of South-east Asia try to rule in a similar way.

Most of the countries are democracies, but the real power of the people to change their governments varies. Voters have little power in Myanmar (Burma), which has a military government. Laos and Vietnam are communist countries, which have only one party to chose from. The heads of state are usually presidents or prime ministers, but Thailand, Cambodia and Malaysia have kings or princes, and Brunei is ruled by a sultan.

Village life
This Vietnamese boy is bringing harvested rice back to his village. Vietnam is the fourth largest producer of rice in the world.

Asian tigers

During the last few decades of the 20th century, some countries in South-east Asia went through a period of rapid change. They began to develop new industries, and built factories to make cars, televisions, computer equipment and clothes. The more successful of these countries – Singapore, Thailand, Indonesia, Malaysia and the Philippines – formed a powerful trading group called the Association of South-east Asian Nations (ASEAN), and were nicknamed 'Asian Tigers'.

In 1997, however, the world economy went into decline, causing great difficulties for these countries. Nonetheless, the ASEAN countries are still the leading industrial nations of the region. Malaysia has rich resources in tin, oil, rubber and timber. Indonesia has copper, oil and gas. Tiny Brunei, which joined ASEAN in 1984, is one of the world's leading oil-producers.

As a result of the boom years, the cities of South-east Asia have also grown fast. The centres of the biggest cities, such as Indonesia's capital Jakarta, are very modern, with air-conditioned office blocks and smart shopping malls. Malaysia's capital, Kuala Lumpur, has the world's tallest building, the Petronas Twin Towers, completed in 1997 and rising to 452 m in 88 floors.

Many people have moved to the cities from the countryside in the hope of finding work. Thousands live in poor shanty towns that cluster around the outskirts of cities such as Jakarta and the Philippine capital, Manila.

Mango farming

Most people in South-east Asia still live in rural areas, making a living by farming – producing rice and a wide range of vegetables and other crops, such as mangoes, coconuts, sugar cane and spices. A large number of people live from the sea, catching fish from trawlers or traditional outrigger sailing canoes carved from the trunks of trees. These food products may be exported, or go to factories specialising in food processing. But many also end up at the lively street markets, full of colour, noise and strong smells.

High rise

The 88-storey Petronas Twin Towers in Malaysia's capital Kuala Lumpur were completed in 1997. They are made of glass, steel and concrete. The two towers are joined at the 41st and 42nd floors (175 m above street level) by a 58.4 m skybridge.

Rice harvest

More than a fifth of the world's rice is grown in South-east Asia. The rice is grown on flooded terraces cut into the hillsides. Much of it is still harvested by hand, which is back-breaking work for the farming communities.

A mosaic of religions

In the past, most people in South-east Asia followed traditional religions, focusing on nature spirits and the spirits of their ancestors. In Thailand, almost every family and business still has a miniature 'spirit house', where daily devotions are made to the guardian spirits.

South-east Asia has a long history as a centre for trade – foreign merchants brought not only goods, but ideas. About 2,000 years ago, Indian traders brought Hinduism to the region. Later, traders and missionaries brought Buddhism, and several powerful empires adopted a mixture of the two, called 'Hindu-Buddhism'. Vast temples were built at Angkor Wat in Cambodia and Borobudur in Indonesia.

In about 1250, Indian traders brought Islam, and it spread throughout many of the islands and into Malaysia. Today, Indonesia has more Muslims than any other country in the world. The small Indonesian island of Bali, however, is predominantly Hindu. Every village has three temples, so there is a total of some 20,000 temples on the island.

The Spanish brought Christianity to the Philippines, and 87 per cent of the population belong to the Roman Catholic Church. Thailand, Myanmar and Laos are mainly Buddhist. Orange-robed Buddhist

Religious mix

These temple-goers are Caodaists. Caodaism has several million followers in Vietnam. It combines elements from many of the world's religions.

Faith schooling

Most people in Indonesia follow Islam and children study the Koran (the holy book of the Muslim world) at school. They learn to recite complex passages by heart.

Hindu offering

This young woman carries an offering to a Hindu temple in Bali. Worship in the temple is led by a priest called a brahman.

monks can be seen in the numerous temples, or collecting food offerings in the street from members of the public. In Thailand, many men at some point in their lives take a few months off work to become temporary monks.

Religion is usually the main focus of the many traditional festivals. Loy Krathong is a Thai festival that takes place at the full moon in November. People float candles on little banana-leaf boats on rivers, ponds and canals in the hope that their prayers will be answered. In the Hindu Thaipusam festival celebrated in Singapore and Malaysia, devotees pierce their bodies with skewers and hooks, apparently without suffering pain.

Importance of education

Education is a high priority in all South-east Asian countries. Most nations in the region have a high 'literacy rate' (the proportion of people who can read and write). In small country villages, and even in the shanty towns that rim the big cities, children go to school every day.

In Bali, children are so highly regarded that their feet are not allowed to touch the ground for the first year of life, and there are special ceremonies to mark every stage of the lives. But not all children in South-east Asia are so lucky. In the big cities, they are often sent out to work, perhaps selling newspapers or cigarettes at traffic lights. Some even work on the rubbish tips, going through piles of stinking garbage in search of anything that can be recycled.

Layers of language

The ancestors of the modern population of South-east Asia came originally from southern China about 5,000 years ago. They brought with them their own languages, such as Malay, Thai, Khmer (Cambodian), Vietnamese and Filipino. But there are many other local languages. Myanmar, for instance, has at least 100 languages besides Burmese.

In Malaysia and Indonesia, traders developed a kind of market language called Bahasa. Today, Bahasa Malaysia and Bahasa Indonesia are the official languages of those countries.

In 1511, the first Europeans arrived in South-east Asia, in search of the precious spices of the 'Spice Islands',

Good results

Although Vietnam is a poor country with a troubled past, it has a high literacy rate. Because education is so important, students have to do a lot of homework.

a group of Indonesian islands called the Moluccas where nutmeg and cloves grow. Soon after, the Dutch, English and Spanish began to take over parts of South-east Asia, and by the end of the 19th century, Thailand was the only country not ruled by a European nation. The British ruled Myanmar, Malaysia and Singapore; the French ruled Cambodia, Laos and Vietnam; the Dutch ruled Indonesia; and the Spanish (and later the USA) ruled the Philippines. The British brought large numbers of Chinese and Indian workers to Malaysia and Singapore, and many of their descendants still live there.

All these countries became independent in the second half of the 20th century, but they retain reminders of this past, seen in government buildings and in the rubber and tea plantations. Malaysia, Singapore and Brunei still belong to the Commonwealth.

Exercise yard

These Vietnamese children are having an exercise class in their school yard. As well as reading and writing, they are taught maths and science, foreign languages and Vietnamese history. The literacy rate in Vietnam is 93%.

Troubled lands

After Vietnam gained independence from France in 1954, the country was divided into two with communists controlling the North. War broke out between North and South. The United States supported South Vietnam and became deeply involved in the conflict. By the time South Vietnam surrendered in 1975, the war had cost the lives of more than 1.5 million Vietnamese.

Cambodia was cast into turmoil when the Khmer Rouge regime, led by Pol Pot, ruled the country from 1975 to 1979. More than two million people (almost a third of the country's total population) were executed or died of famine during this time.

On parade

Smartly dressed in their school uniforms, these Vietnamese girls are visiting the tomb of communist leader Ho Chi Minh on the date of his birthday, which is a national holiday.

Sporting nations

Football is played throughout South-east Asia. Badminton is a big sport in Indonesia and baseball is popular in the Philippines. There are also more traditional sports and games. Takraw or chin-lon is similar to football and is played with a rattan (cane) ball. Thai-boxing, in which kicking is allowed, is practised in Thailand. Competitive kite-flying takes place throughout Thailand, Malaysia and Indonesia. In some kite-flying events, contestants stick powdered glass to the line to try to saw through the lines of rival kite-flyers.

Puppets, dancing and arts

When Hinduism arrived in South-east Asia, it was adopted first of all by the royal courts. As in India, temple ceremonies were accompanied by elaborate dancing designed to please the gods. Complex and ornate forms of dancing developed, especially in Thailand and in Indonesia, and these traditions continue to this day. In Indonesia, gamelan orchestras, made up almost entirely of xylophones, accompany the dancers.

Shadow puppets were used to relate tales from the great Hindu epics, and puppetry remains a popular form of entertainment, both in Indonesia and Malaysia. With just a flaming oil lamp, a screen made from a sheet of white material, and a box full of puppets cut in silhouette out of leather, skilled puppeteers can hold an audience spellbound with love-stories, clowning and giant battle scenes, complete with flying arrows and lances.

Temple dance
Colourfully dressed young dancers perform a graceful routine in Angkor Wat, a magnificent Hindu temple in Cambodia.

There are hundreds of gifted sculptors and painters across the region. They decorate the Buddhist temples of Thailand and the huge houses of the Toraja people on the Indonesian island of Sulawesi, and carve masks, fruits, animals and statues of the gods in Bali.

In the Philippines, the jeepneys (jeep-like taxis) are decorated from top to bottom, inside and out, with paintings, stickers, sculptures, lights and tassels.

Tourism is an important source of income in South-east Asia. The region can offer everything from luxury beach resorts to treks in the remote rainforests of Borneo. Indonesia alone receives over 4.5 million tourists every year.

BRUNEI

Capital
Bandar Seri Begawan
Area
5,765 km²
Population
331,000
Population density
54 per km²
Life expectancy
70 (m); 73 (f)
Religions
Islam, Buddhism, Christianity
Languages
Malay, Chinese, English
Adult literacy rate
89 per cent
Currency
Brunei dollar

 CAMBODIA

Capital
Phnom Penh
Area
181,035 km²
Population
10,945,000
Population density
63 per km²
Life expectancy
50 (m); 52 (f)
Religions
Buddhism, Islam
Language
Khmer
Adult literacy rate
35 per cent
Currency
riel

 CHINA

Capital
Beijing
Area
9,571,300 km²
Population
1,274,115,000
Population density
132 per km²
Life expectancy
66 (m); 70 (f)
Religions
Confucianism, Taoism,
Buddhism, Christianity, Islam
Languages
Northern Chinese (Mandarin
or Putonghua), Min, Wu, Yue
(Cantonese) and others
Adult literacy rate
82 per cent
Currency
yuan, Hong Kong dollar and
Macau pataca

Population control

China's population was growing so fast that the communist government introduced a policy of penalising families who had more than one child. This law has been relaxed in recent years.

Rocky grave

This graveyard in Indonesia is carved into the rock face. Balconies of tau tau (small wooden statues representing grave guardians) stand watch.

 EAST TIMOR

Capital
Dili
Area
14,609 km²
Population
920,000
Population density
63 per km²
Life expectancy
49 (m); 50 (f)
Religions
Islam, Christianity
Languages
Indonesian (Bahasa Indonesia, a form of Malay), Portuguese, Timor, Tetun and other local languages
Adult literacy rate
15 per cent
Currency
US dollar

 INDONESIA

Capital
Jakarta
Area
1,904,708 km²
Population
207,437,000
Population density
108 per km²
Life expectancy
61 (m); 64 (f)
Religions
Islam, Christianity, Hinduism, Buddhism
Languages
Indonesian (Bahasa Indonesia, a form of Malay) and local languages
Adult literacy rate
84 per cent
Currency
rupiah

 JAPAN

Capital
Tokyo
Area
377,750 km²
Population
126,505,000
Population density
335 per km²
Life expectancy
76 (m); 83 (f)
Religions
Shintoism, Buddhism
Language
Japanese
Adult literacy rate
99 per cent
Currency
yen

 **LAOS**

Capital
Vientiane
Area
236,800 km²
Population
5,297,000
Population density
22 per km²
Life expectancy
49 (m); 52 (f)
Religions
Buddhism, traditional beliefs
Languages
Lao (Laotian), French and
many local languages
Adult literacy rate
57 per cent
Currency
new kip

MALAYSIA

Capital
Kuala Lumpur
Area
329,758 km²
Population
22,712,000
Population density
67 per km²
Life expectancy
68 (m); 73 (f)
Religions
Islam, Buddhism
Languages
Malay (Bahasa Malaysia),
English, Chinese, Tamil, Iban
Adult literacy rate
83 per cent
Currency
ringgit

 **MONGOLIA**

Capital
Ulan Bator
Area
1,566,500 km²
Population
2,383,000
Population density
2 per km²
Life expectancy
62 (m); 65 (f)
Religion
Buddhism
Languages
Khalkha, Mongolian, Kazakh
Adult literacy rate
83 per cent
Currency
tugrik

Tent life
*Outside of the big towns and cities, many nomadic
Mongolians chose to live in traditional gers (tents).*

MYANMAR

Capital
Yangon (Rangoon)
Area
676,553 km²
Population
45,059,000
Population density
71 per km²
Life expectancy
57 (m); 63 (f)
Religions
Buddhism, Christianity, Islam
Languages
Myanmar (Burmese) and other local languages
Adult literacy rate
83 per cent
Currency
kyat

NORTH KOREA

Capital
Pyongyang
Area
120,538 km²
Population
23,702,000
Population density
194 per km²
Life expectancy
68 (m); 74 (f)
Religions
Ch'ondogyo (combines elements of Roman Catholicism, Buddhism, Taoism and Shamanism), traditional beliefs,
Language
Korean
Adult literacy rate
99 per cent
Currency
North Korean won

PHILIPPINES

Capital
Manila
Area
300,000 km²
Population
74,746,000
Population density
251 per km²
Life expectancy
63 (m); 67 (f)
Religions
Christianity, Islam
Languages
Filipino, English and other local languages
Adult literacy rate
95 per cent
Currency
Philippine peso

SINGAPORE

Capital
Singapore
Area
646 km²
Population
3,894,000
Population density
5,991 per km²
Life expectancy
74 (m); 78 (f)
Religions
Buddhism, Taoism, Islam, Christianity, Hinduism
Languages Malay, Chinese (Mandarin), Tamil, English
Adult literacy rate
91 per cent
Currency
Singapore dollar

SOUTH KOREA

Capital
Seoul
Area
99,392 km²
Population
46,858,000
Population density
467 per km²
Life expectancy
67 (m); 75 (f)
Religions
Buddhism, Christianity
Language
Korean
Adult literacy rate
98 per cent
Currency
South Korean won

 TAIWAN

Capital
Taipei
Area
36,000 km²
Population
21,740,000
Population density
604 per km²
Life expectancy
72 (m); 78 (f)
Religions
Taoism, Buddhism
Languages
Northern Chinese (Mandarin),
Taiwanese
Adult literacy rate
94 per cent
Currency
Taiwan dollar

 THAILAND

Capital
Bangkok
Area
513,115 km²
Population
60,607,000
Population density
119 per km²
Life expectancy
64 (m); 69 (f)
Religions
Buddhism, Islam
Languages
Thai, Chinese, Malay
Adult literacy rate
94 per cent
Currency
baht

Vietnam

*Winters are cold in
northern Vietnam,
so this mother has
dressed her young
children in
warm clothes.*

 VIETNAM

Capital
Hanoi
Area
331,114 km²
Population
76,325,000
Population density
234 per km²
Life expectancy
63 (m); 67 (f)
Religions
Taoism, Buddhism,
Christianity
Languages
Vietnamese and local
languages
Adult literacy rate
94 per cent
Currency
dông

Australia

New Zealand

Pacific Islands

AUSTRALIA AND THE PACIFIC

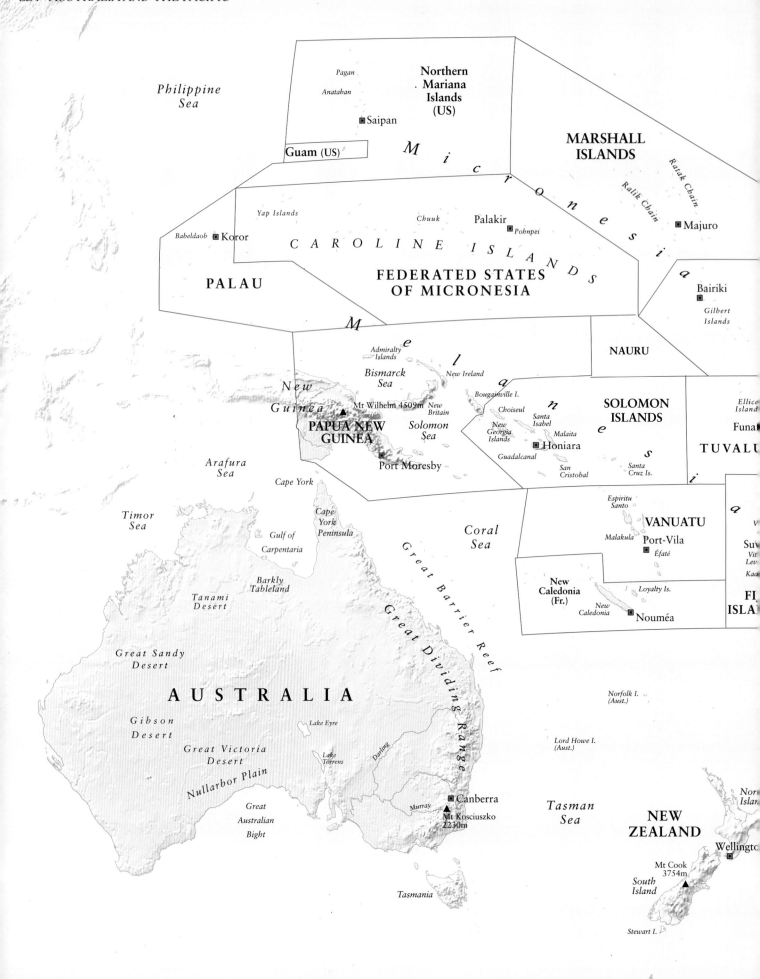

Philippine Sea

Pagan

Anatahan

Northern Mariana Islands (US)

Saipan

MARSHALL ISLANDS

Ratak Chain

Ralik Chain

M i c r o n e s i a

Guam (US)

Yap Islands

Chuuk

Palakir

Pohnpei

Majuro

C A R O L I N E   I S L A N D S

Babeldaob Koror

PALAU

FEDERATED STATES OF MICRONESIA

Bairiki

Gilbert Islands

M e l a n e s i a

NAURU

Admiralty Islands

Bismarck Sea

New Ireland

Bougainville I.

SOLOMON ISLANDS

Ellice Island

New Guinea

Mt Wilhelm 4509m New Britain

Choiseul

Santa Isabel

Funa

PAPUA NEW GUINEA

Solomon Sea

New Georgia Islands

Malaita

Honiara

TUVALU

Port Moresby

Guadalcanal

San Cristobal

Santa Cruz Is.

Arafura Sea

Cape York

Coral Sea

Espiritu Santo

VANUATU

Timor Sea

Cape York Peninsula

Malakula

Port-Vila

Éfaté

Suv

Fi

Vit

Lev

Kaa

FI

ISLA

Gulf of Carpentaria

New Caledonia (Fr.)

Loyalty Is.

Barkly Tableland

New Caledonia

Nouméa

Tanami Desert

Great Sandy Desert

Great Dividing Range

Great Barrier Reef

Norfolk I. (Aust.)

AUSTRALIA

Gibson Desert

Lake Eyre

Lord Howe I. (Aust.)

Great Victoria Desert

Lake Torrens

Darling

Tasman Sea

Nullarbor Plain

Murray

Canberra

Nor

Islan

NEW ZEALAND

Great Australian Bight

Mt Kosciuszko 2230m

Wellingto

Mt Cook 3754m

Tasmania

South Island

Stewart I.

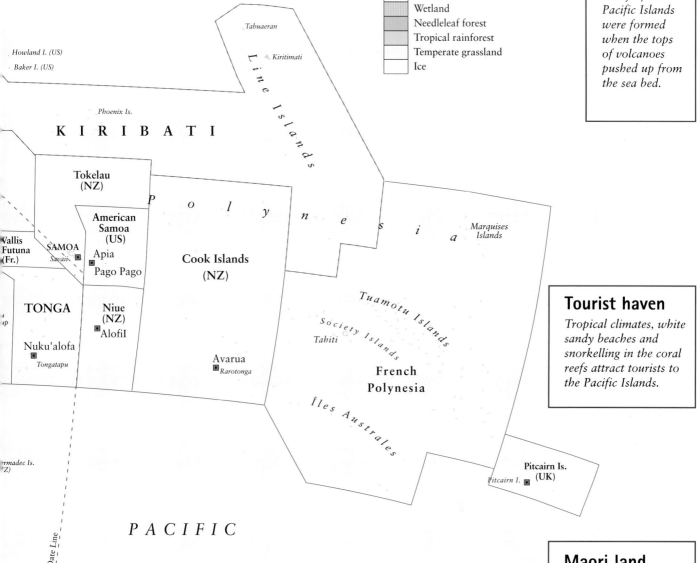

Hawaiian
Islands
(US)

PACIFIC

OCEAN

Mountain
Desert
Tundra
Cropland
Wetland
Needleleaf forest
Tropical rainforest
Temperate grassland
Ice

Palmyra (US)

Tabuaeran

Kiritimati

Howland I. (US)

Baker I. (US)

Line Islands

Phoenix Is.

K I R I B A T I

**Tokelau
(NZ)**

P   o   l   y   n   e   s   i   a

*Marquises
Islands*

**American
Samoa
(US)**

Wallis
Futuna
(Fr.)

SAMOA
Savaii

Apia
Pago Pago

**Cook Islands
(NZ)**

Tuamotu Islands

TONGA

**Niue
(NZ)**
AlofiI

Society Islands
Tahiti

up

Nuku'alofa
Tongatapu

Avarua
Rarotonga

**French
Polynesia**

Îles Australes

*rmadec Is.
Z)*

Pitcairn I.

**Pitcairn Is.
(UK)**

PACIFIC

OCEAN

International Date Line

*hatham Is.
Z)*

| 0 | 1000 | 2000 km |
| 0 | 500 | 1000 miles |

N

City life

Over 85 per cent of the Australian population lives in cities. The biggest is Sydney, but the capital is Canberra.

Volcanic islands

Many of the Pacific Islands were formed when the tops of volcanoes pushed up from the sea bed.

Tourist haven

Tropical climates, white sandy beaches and snorkelling in the coral reefs attract tourists to the Pacific Islands.

Maori land

Maoris were the first settlers in New Zealand, 1,200 years ago. Most of today's inhabitants are descended from British migrants.

AUSTRALIA

Australians sometimes refer to their homeland as 'the lucky country'. It has sunny weather most of the year, with fine beaches and warm blue seas. There is plenty of fertile land, a wealth of natural resources and an energetic, resourceful population. Australians pride themselves on living well and enjoying life.

Australia is vast – the sixth largest country in the world – but very little of the land is inhabited. The population stands at just 18.9 million, which, averaged out over the entire surface area of Australia, means that there are fewer than three people per km^2. Most people live close to the coast in the south-east. This is where three of the largest cities lie – Sydney, Melbourne, and Brisbane. Another large city, Perth, is 3,000 km away on the west coast. Much of what lies between the west coast and the east coast is desert – hot, dry plains of sand and gravel. The only town in the 'red centre' of Australia (so-called because of the colour of the desert soil) is Alice Springs.

Red rocks

The impressive red mountains of the Olgas, in the Australian outback, are considered sacred by the Aboriginal people.

Flying farmers

In Australia's hot and humid north, farmers grow sugar cane and tropical fruits. In the cooler south, they grow wheat and potatoes, and the grapes that are used to make Australia's world-famous wines.

In the great belts of scrubland and bush in the remote 'outback', which lies between the coastal regions and the desert, there are huge livestock farms, where large flocks of sheep and herds of cattle are raised. A single sheep farm may cover 5,000 km². These farms are so big that the farm workers sometimes use small aircraft to check their herds, and stockmen get around using motorbikes and quad-bikes.

Families running the farms often live far from the nearest neighbours or towns. Because they are so far from any school, children are taught at home, with lessons conducted by the 'School of the Air', on two-way radios or over the internet. If they are ill, the 'flying doctor' arrives by plane.

Farming plays an important

Herds of cattle
A few cattle stations in southern Australia are larger than some countries – up to 30,000 km².

part in Australia's wealth. With its 160 million sheep, it produces a quarter of the world's wool. But less than five per cent of the Australian workforce is employed in agriculture. Others work in manufacturing, car production, electrical goods and textiles, or in the service industries such as banking and finance.

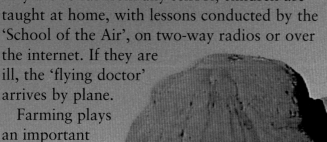

Who are the Australians?

When Captain Cook raised his flag at Botany Bay, just south of Sydney, in 1770 and claimed Australia for England, he knew very little about the people already living there. In fact there were some 600 native groups, with about 300 separate languages. They became known simply as the Aboriginals (from the Latin *ab origine*, 'from the beginning'). Their ancestors had come to Australia at least 40,000 years before.

Each group had developed its own way of life, according to its surroundings – which differed hugely from the tropical north to the cool mountains of the island of Tasmania in the far south. They lived by hunting and fishing, using spears, nets and boomerangs, and by gathering edible plants, nuts, fruit and insect grubs (such as the large and nutritious witchetty grubs). They traded goods including stone tools, natural dyes and precious shells right across the continent. As a result, they developed an intimate knowledge of the land and its wildlife, and built this into their religious beliefs and their myths and legends.

European settlers

This ancient pattern of life suddenly came under threat after Captain Cook's visit. In 1788, the British sent their first shipload of European settlers to Australia. At first, these were criminals, sent to Australia as a punishment – often for minor crimes such as poaching or picking pockets. In all, over 160,000 criminals were 'transported' to Australia, and many stayed on to make a living as farmers. Other European settlers also came to Australia, making new lives for themselves in the fertile lands and new cities.

The Aboriginal people were powerless to stop the Europeans. They had only primitive weapons, and little resistance to the diseases that the Europeans brought with them, such as measles. The Europeans took their land, introduced completely new ways of life, such as sheep-farming, and many Aboriginal people were killed. The total number of Aboriginal people fell rapidly, from about 300,000 in the 1770s to just 70,000 in the 1930s.

Preserving traditions

Since that time, the Aboriginal people have been better treated and their numbers have increased to 200,000 – but this is only 1.5 per cent of the total population.

Aboriginal art

Aboriginal artists drew pictures in the sand, on trees and, like this one, rock surfaces. Traditionally, they used brushes made from sticks that had been chewed until the ends were frayed.

The Aboriginal people are anxious to preserve their traditions, such as the sacred rituals of music-making and body-painting. Aboriginal people believe the land is a sacred place with unseen spiritual forces, and natural landmarks such as mountains and trees are treated as holy sites. They also keep alive stories about the 'Dreamtime' – a distant time when they believe the landscape came into being. Their traditional dot-paintings, often depict the mythical Dreamtime creatures.

In recent decades, the Aboriginal people have had some success in claiming back large tracts of their land from the Australian government, and now control how this land is used.

An international land

The population of newer Australian settlers has changed significantly. Up until about 50 years ago, most of them came from Europe, and mainly from Britain and Ireland. After World War II, a large number of immigrants came from Greece, Italy and Turkey. More recently, there has been an influx of immigrants from Asia.

As a result, Australia's cities are a melting pot of cultures. Immigrant communities have brought with them their own religions, festivals and foods. Sydney, for example, is famous for its great range of restaurants, serving cuisine from all around the world.

New generation

Although many Aboriginal people still live in the outback, the majority now live in towns. Aboriginal people are very proud of their culture and traditions and pass them on to their children.

Sun, sand and sport

More than 80 per cent of Australians live in towns along the coast, within easy reach of the beach. They make the most of their sunny climate – swimming, surfing, sailing or simply enjoying a barbecue all year round. Possibly because of their outdoor lifestyle, the Australians are superb at sports. Just think of Shane Warne (cricket), Cathy Freeman (athletics) or Lleyton Hewitt (tennis).

Rules of the game

These boys are playing a type of rugby called Australian Rules. It is played with an oval ball on an oval pitch.

Wildlife wonders

Cut adrift from the rest of the world, Australia is home to some very unusual animals. Kangaroos, wombats, wallabies and koalas are all marsupials (mammals with a pocket, or pouch, on their stomach for carrying and nursing babies). The country's unique animal kingdom includes the platypus and the echidna, the only mammals that lay eggs. There are also some highly dangerous creatures such as sharks, jellyfish, the saltwater crocodile and some of the most poisonous snakes and spiders in the world.

King crab

Two children enjoy the beach, in the company of a giant king crab, one of the world's largest crabs.

A people apart

Australia has strong links with Britain. The main language is English – although Australian English has distinctive touches, with its own accent, and words such as tucker (food), dinkum (genuine) and the greeting 'G'day' (good day). Most of the institutions, including the education and justice systems, are based on British models. Queen Elizabeth II is the head of state and is represented in Australia by the governor-general. However, a growing number of Australians want their country to break free of the historic ties with Britain, and to become a republic, headed by a president rather that the British monarch. In 1999, the Australians voted by a narrow majority to stay loyal to the queen.

Australia's outlook on the world is changing. Increasingly, as trade and cultural links develop with closer neighbouring countries such as Japan, China and the Pacific Islands, Australians see themselves more as part of the Pacific than as part of distant Europe – which, after all, lies on the other side of the globe.

Dramatic view

Sydney is Australia's financial and business centre. The bridge and opera house in Sydney's harbour are very popular tourist attractions.

National identity

Although the Australian flag contains Britain's Union Jack, many in Australia believe it is time the country left behind its colonial roots.

NEW ZEALAND

Lying in the South Pacific Ocean, 1,600 km south-east of Australia, New Zealand is a land of snow-capped mountains and volcanoes, of gurgling rivers and still lakes, deep forests and lush pasture, and dramatic, rocky coastlines. It is divided into two large islands, called the North Island and the South Island, and a smattering of smaller islands.

Kiwis

Agriculture is New Zealand's primary industry. Highly geared towards export markets, it uses modern and efficient farming methods. From herds of dairy cattle, farmers produce New Zealand's famous butter and cheese and the sheep provide wool and meat. The well-watered pastures are able to support large herds, with high yields of milk, meat and wool. New Zealand has a population of 3.8 million, but its sheep population is estimated to be 45 million.

Forestry is another important industry. Conifer trees are grown for timber, chipboard and to make paper. Fishing for lobsters, crayfish, oysters and numerous other kinds of seafood also provides valuable exports.

Sheep farming

New Zealand's lush pastures are perfect for sheep farming. Sheep were first brought to the country by Captain Cook in 1773.

In recent years, New Zealand has become famous for another export – a fruit developed in the North Island from a Chinese berry that grows on thick vines. Once called a Chinese gooseberry, it is now better known as a kiwi fruit. 'Kiwi' is also the nickname for New Zealanders generally – taken from the name of a flightless bird, unique to the country.

City life

Only 15 per cent of New Zealanders live in the country. The rest live in the towns and cities. The biggest city is Auckland, in the north of the North Island. It is also the country's main port. The capital, Wellington, is in the south of the North Island. High-rise offices front the harbour in the financial and administrative centre, but the windy and earthquake-prone hillsides behind are dotted with timber houses.

Although larger, the colder, more mountainous South Island has a smaller population than North Island, from which it is separated by the 26-km-wide Cook Strait. The South Island's largest city is Christchurch.

Kiwi capital

Kiwi fruit grow on vines. The brown fuzzy skin covers emerald-green flesh dotted with edible black seeds. They were brought to New Zealand by Chinese missionaries at the beginning of the 20th century.

Maoris

The first settlers in New Zealand, the Maoris, arrived in sailing canoes from the Polynesian islands to the north in about AD 800. Captain Cook mapped the islands in 1769, and whalers, fur-traders and Christian missionaries began to settle on the coasts in the next century. Under the Treaty of Waitangi in 1840, the British persuaded Maori tribal chiefs to hand over their sovereignty, in return for guarantees that protected ownership of their lands. But the British side of the bargain was quickly broken. New Zealand became a British colony and settlers began pouring in.

By the end of the 19th century, the Maoris had been decimated by warfare and disease. But their fortunes recovered, and now pure-blood Maoris and the descendants of mixed marriages make up 14 per cent of the population. In recent years new immigrants from South Pacific islands – notably from Samoa, Fiji, Tonga and the Cook Islands – have settled in New Zealand.

The Maoris still preserve their traditional ways of life in some areas of the North Island,

Cultural tradition

Maoris remember their roots by teaching children the history of the Maoris and about the particular group they belong to.

such as the region of volcanic springs around Rotorua, where houses are decorated with fine wooden carvings and statues of the protective gods sticking out their tongues in the traditional Maori greeting. The government has returned tribal lands to the Maoris and Maori, now an official language of New Zealand, is taught in the country's schools.

Volcanic landscape

Rotorua is a volcanic region on the North Island. It is covered in steaming craters, boiling mud pools and geysers spouting hot steam.

All Blacks

The haka (the Maori warrior dance) is performed by New Zealand's national rugby union team, the All Blacks (so-called because they wear a black kit). They are one of the world's greatest rugby teams, producing international stars such as Jonah Lomu.

New Zealanders are also enthusiastic cricketers and yachtsmen, and they have excellent skiing facilities. Bowls is a popular pastime, especially among older people. The open spaces at the centre of many towns are often squared off with neatly mown bowling greens.

Rugby giant

All Blacks' star Jonah Lomu is one of the most famous rugby players in the world and a national hero in New Zealand.

New links

Many aspects of New Zealand life reflect its connections to Britain, and the British monarch is the head of state. In recent years there has been a decline in trade with Britain, and New Zealand has had to look elsewhere for export markets. It has developed closer trade links with other nations in the Pacific region and Asia.

New Zealand is a key member of the Pacific Islands Forum, and has supported the drive to make the region 'nuclear-free'. New Zealand does not have nuclear power. Instead electricity is generated mainly by hydroelectric power.

PACIFIC ISLANDS

Idyllic islands

French Polynesia attracts many visitors with its stylish holiday resorts and beautiful lagoons teeming with tropical fish.

Dotted across the vast, blue Pacific Ocean are some 25,000 islands, many of them tiny. The nations of the region are mostly made up of island groups scattered across a large area of sea. Tonga, for example, consists of two large islands and about 150 smaller ones. The islands include some of the world's smallest nations – Nauru is just 21 km².

Excluding New Zealand there are 12 independent countries in the region, but some island groups remain dependent on other larger countries. For instance, the large island of New Caledonia is a French territory, as is French Polynesia, which includes Tahiti. Hawaii is a US state, and Guam and American Samoa (not to be confused with neighbouring Samoa, which is independent) are US territories. Northern Marianas is also closely associated with the USA. The tiny island of Pitcairn is a British territory, and Easter Island belongs to Chile, a South American country.

Three groups

In the 1800s, the islands of the South Pacific were divided by geographers into three groups – Melanesia, Polynesia and Micronesia. Melanesia consists of the larger islands in the southwest of the region – Papua New Guinea, the Solomon Islands, Vanuatu and Fiji. They are inhabited by people whose ancestors travelled to the islands from South-east Asia about 40,000 years ago. They developed a way of life based upon growing yams and raising pigs – still the basis of farming in many of the islands today.

Over time, new waves of people headed further east in search of new islands to settle. They travelled in large sailing canoes to the islands now called Polynesia, which include Hawaii, Easter Island, Tuvalu, Samoa and Tonga. The Polynesians had their own language, gods and ways of life, creating a distinctive and connected culture – all the more remarkable because it covered such a vast area. The Polynesians were impressive navigators. They used their knowledge of the winds, the stars and the flight patterns of seabirds to find their way from island to island across vast areas of open sea. Many islanders still have these skills, and use them to move around the ocean, often in wooden outrigger sailing canoes, whose design has changed little for hundreds of years.

The third group is Micronesia, a peppering of small islands or island groups which spreads most of the way across the central belt of the Pacific. Palau, the Federated States of Micronesia, the Marshall Islands, Nauru and Kiribati make up Micronesia.

Island dancer

Dancing is an important cultural tradition to the people of Micronesia. Men and women dance in separate groups and the dancing is often accompanied by unison chanting.

Foreign influences

European explorers and traders first visited the Pacific Islands over 300 years ago. Christian missionaries came to the region from the late 1700s, and most islands are now Christian. During the 19th century, Britain, France, Germany and the USA took over many of the islands as colonies. They developed huge plantations, growing crops such as sugar and pineapples.

The British created huge sugar-cane plantations in Fiji, and brought in people from India to work in them. Now nearly half the population of Fiji is Asian.

Nauru, once a British colony, had rich deposits of phosphate – seabird dung – which was extracted and sold as fertiliser.

Worship

More than half of the people of Fiji are Christian. Music and choir-singing form a large part of worship in the country's churches.

Most of this has now gone, but Nauru still lives off the profits, which were carefully invested abroad, notably in property in Australia.

Since winning their independence in the 20th century, the islands have been looking for ways to support their economies in the long term. Most of them have only limited natural resources, and plantation crops do not provide big profits. One new major source of income is fishing. Countries such as the USA, Japan, Korea and Taiwan pay large sums of money to many of the Pacific nations for permission to fish in their waters.

Cyclones and volcanoes

The Pacific Islands straddle the equator and they have a hot, humid climate. The more mountainous islands receive plenty of rain, which drops when the moisture-laden clouds rise up the hills and cool.

Every year the heat over the ocean stirs the air into a spiralling funnel of very strong winds, called cyclones. They move across the region, ripping up everything in their path.

Another danger comes from deep beneath the earth. The Pacific Islands cover a very unstable part of the earth's crust, where

Stormy lands

The Pacific Islanders often have to cope with cyclones ripping apart their towns and villages.

tectonic plates are slowly colliding. This pushes up volcanoes, and causes earthquakes and tsunamis (fast, destructive waves).

In fact, many Pacific Islands are volcanic in origin. They were formed when the tops of volcanoes pushed up from the seabed.

However, volcanoes, earthquakes and tsunamis can cause destruction, sometimes wiping out entire villages, killing many and leaving survivors without food or homes.

Natural riches

Volcanoes create very rich soil. This, combined with plenty of warmth and rain, means that plants generally grow very well in the Pacific region. Many of the islanders grow their own fruit and vegetables in gardens next to their villages. They produce yams, papayas, coconuts and pumpkins. Fishermen make good catches in the still, shallow lagoons created by coral reefs, or in the deep sea beyond the reefs, bringing in sea perch, shark and tuna.

Coconut palms provide wood and leaves to make simple thatched houses. Villages in Samoa, for instance, consist of very simple, open-sided dwellings, like roofed platforms, raised above the ground on stones. This design suits the hot and humid climate well. Walls of matting are used only to keep out troublesome breezes. There is very little furniture and people sleep on mats. Villages are closely knit and sociable, usually formed around families and clans, and run by village headmen and a council of elders.

Ocean wonderland

The seas of the Pacific Ocean are home to beautiful coral reefs and abundant and varied sea life including tropical fish and sponges.

Heavy load

Villagers in Papua New Guinea carry firewood in bilum bags strapped to their heads. The bags are made from sago palm leaves.

On the smaller islands, the sea is never far away. On the larger islands there are high volcanic hills, tropical forests and remote plains and river valleys. In some Melanesian islands there are peoples living far inland who have had very little contact with the outside world. Over the centuries these isolated villages developed their own languages, with the result that Papua New Guinea has more than 800 languages and the Solomons have over 70. Many people in this region also speak pidgin, a shared language used for trading.

Ancient and modern

The long-isolated communities of Melanesia still preserve many aspects of their individual cultures. In northern Papua New Guinea, for instance, the people of the Sepik river area produce sacred carvings of their ancestor spirits and make masks to use in ritual dances. Many villages have elaborately carved cult-centres or 'spirit houses', where only men are allowed. In the highlands, clans gather for festivals of music and dance, wearing extravagant outfits made of grasses, shells, beads, feathers and body paint. But these days the adornments may also be made of crushed tin cans, and some participants arrive by jeep.

Each year, as part of a festival after the yam harvest in the Pentecost Islands of Vanuatu, young men throw themselves off 25-m-high wooden towers, with their ankles attached to long vines – the original bungee jumping.

One unusual effect of long isolation was the development of 'cargo cults' in Melanesia, particularly in Vanuatu. Whole religions, mixing local myths and Christianity, grew up around foreign messiah figures who magically brought rich cargoes of goods by ship or plane.

The capital cities of many of the Pacific Island nations are quite modern. They have airports, satellite links, bus services, air-conditioned buildings and international banks. But the islanders still follow many traditions. For instance, the men and women of Tonga still wear stiff ta'ovala skirts made of woven pandanus palm mats. The people of Tonga, Fiji and Samoa wear felt-like tapa cloth, made from the pounded bark of mulberry trees and painted with patterns. The mildly narcotic drink kava, prepared from the root of a pepper plant, is still drunk with informal ceremony in Vanuatu, Fiji, Samoa and Tonga, and some islands of Micronesia.

Hopes for tourism

Most of the islands are very small, and many people leave to make new lives for themselves in New Zealand, Australia or the USA. There

Beauty contest
As part of one Papua New Guinea festival, women take part in a beauty contest. As well as for beauty, they are judged on skills in body painting and dancing.

are 80,000 Pacific Islanders in Australia alone.

Meanwhile, more visitors are coming to the region – but this time on holiday. The Pacific Islands represent a tourist dream, of white sand beaches, blue seas, warm sun and idyllic cottages beneath the coconut palms. Fiji, in particular, is developing its tourist facilities, and now receives about 350,000 visitors a year. Tourists come to stay in the large resorts, but also to trek in the tropical forests, climb volcanoes, dive among the coral reefs and sail to remote islands.

Tourism brings valuable foreign income to the islands, and the nations of the Pacific Islands want to use tourism as a means of promoting and strengthening their own culture. Tourism gives them a reason to preserve their traditions of dance and music, cooking, basket-weaving and wood-carving.

Tourism hopes

Many of the Pacific Island nations see tourism as an important source of income and are developing their tourist facilties.

AUSTRALIA

Capital
Canberra
Area
7,682,300 km²
Population
18,967,000
Population density
2 per km²
Life expectancy
75 (m); 80 (f)
Religion
Christianity
Languages
English, plus about 200
Aboriginal and many
European and Asian languages
Adult literacy rate
95 per cent
Currency
Australian dollar

FEDERATED STATES OF MICRONESIA

Capital
Palikir, on Pohnpei
Area
700 km²
Population
116,000
Population density
157 per km²
Life expectancy
71 (m); 71 (f)
Religion
Christianity
Languages
English, Trukese, Pohnpeian,
Yapese
Adult literacy rate
90 per cent
Currency
US dollar

FIJI

Capital
Suva, on Viti Levu
Area
18,376 km²
Population
806,000
Population density
44 per km²
Life expectancy
70 (m); 74 (f)
Religions
Christianity, Hinduism,
Sikhism, Islam
Languages
Fijian, Hindi, English
Adult literacy rate
92 per cent
Currency
Fiji dollar

Rocky land

Australia is home to some striking landscapes. These strange rock formations are in the Pinnacles Desert, Western Australia.

KIRIBATI

Capital
Bairiki, on Tarawa
Area
810 km²
Population
82,000
Population density
100 per km²
Life expectancy
58 (m); 58 (f)
Religion
Christianity
Languages
I-Kiribati (Gilbertese), English
Adult literacy rate
90 per cent
Currency
Australian dollar

MARSHALL ISLANDS

Capital
Dalap-Uliga-Darrit, on Majuro
Area
180 km²
Population
61,000
Population density
339 per km²
Life expectancy
64 (m); 68 (f)
Religion
Christianity
Languages
English, Marshallese, Japanese
Adult literacy rate
91 per cent
Currency
US dollar

NAURU

Capital
No official capital
Area
21 km²
Population
11,000
Population density
516 per km²
Life expectancy
57 (m); 65 (f)
Religion
Christianity
Languages
Nauruan, English
Adult literacy rate
99 per cent
Currency
Australian dollar

NEW ZEALAND

Capital
Wellington
Area
270,534 km²
Population
3,811,000
Population density
14 per km²
Life expectancy
73 (m); 79 (f)
Religion
Christianity
Languages
English, Maori
Adult literacy rate
99 per cent
Currency
New Zealand dollar

PALAU

Capital
Koror, on Koror island
Area
508 km²
Population
18,000
Population density
39 per km²
Life expectancy
60 (m); 63 (f)
Religion
Christianity
Languages
Palauan, English
Adult literacy rate
92 per cent
Currency
US dollar

PAPUA NEW GUINEA

Capital
Port Moresby
Area
462,840 km²
Population
4,702,000
Population density
10 per km²
Life expectancy
55 (m); 57 (f)
Religion
Christianity
Languages
English, Motu, Pidgin and many local languages
Adult literacy rate
72 per cent
Currency
kina

SAMOA

Capital
Apia, on Upolu
Area
2,831 km²
Population
169,000
Population density
59 per km²
Life expectancy
64 (m); 70 (f)
Religion
Christianity
Languages
Samoan, English
Adult literacy rate
97 per cent
Currency
tala

SOLOMON ISLANDS

Capital
Honiara, on Guadalcanal
Area
27,556 km²
Population
430,000
Population density
15 per km²
Life expectancy
68 (m); 73 (f)
Religion
Christianity
Languages
English, Melanesian, Pidgin
and other local languages
Adult literacy rate
60 per cent
Currency
Solomon Islands dollar

TONGA

Capital
Nuku'alofa, on Tongatapu
Area
748 km²
Population
98,000
Population density
134 per km²
Life expectancy
66 (m); 70 (f)
Religion
Christianity
Languages
Tongan, English
Adult literacy rate
93 per cent
Currency
pa'anga

TUVALU

Capital
Vaiaku, on Funafuti
Area
26 km²
Population
11,000
Population density
383 per km²
Life expectancy
64 (m); 69 (f)
Religion
Christianity
Languages
Tuvaluan, English
Adult literacy rate
95 per cent
Currency
Tuvalu dollar

VANUATU

Capital
Vila, on Efate
Area
12,190 km²
Population
186,000
Population density
15 per km²
Life expectancy
63 (m); 67 (f)
Religion
Christianity
Languages
Bislama, English, French and
local languages
Adult literacy rate
53 per cent
Currency
vatu

INDEX

ACKNOWLEDGEMENTS

1 Robert Harding. 2-3 Still Pictures/Neil Cooper. 4-5 Still Pictures/Harmut Schwarzbach. 6-7 Anderson Geographics. 8-9 Robert Harding. 10 Trip/A. Tovy: T; Robert Harding/Gavin Hellier: B. 11 Hutchison Library/ John Wright. 12 Robert Harding/Wally Herbert. 13 Anderson Geographics. 14-15 Still Pictures/Michael Sewell. 15 Still Pictures/Brian & Cherry Alexander. 16 Robert Harding/F. Jackson. 17 Robert Harding/Rover PH/Explorer. 18-19 Anderson Geographics. 20-21 Robert Harding/Gavin Hellier. 21 Hutchison Library/ Andrew Sole. 22 Hutchison Library/Billie Rafaeli. 22-23 Still Pictures/Brian & Cherry Alexander. 24 Trip/V. Kolpakov. 24-25 Trip/J. Greenberg. 26-27 Robert Harding/Roy Rainford. 27 John Meek. 28 Robert Harding/Adam Woolfitt: T; Hutchison Library/ Nancy Durrell McKenna: B. 29 Collections/Graeme Peacock. 30-31 Still Pictures/Ron Giling. 31 Trip/B. Turner. 32 Hutchison Library: L; Trip: R. 33 Still Pictures/Thomas Raupach. 34-35 Rex Features/Sipa Press. 35 Trip/A. Tovy. 36-37 Still Pictures/Thomas Raupach. 37 Still Pictures/Wim Van Cappellen. 38 Hutchison Library: T; Trip/C. Gibson: B. 39 Trip/J.D. Dallet. 40-41 View Pictures/ Dennis Gilbert. 41 Hutchison Library/Edward Parker. 42-43 Still Pictures/ Pierre Gleizes. 43 Still Pictures/ Mark Edwards. 44 Corbis/ Owen Franklin, T; Corbis/ Vittoriano Rastelli, B. 45 Still Pictures/Calvert/UNEP. 46-47 Hutchison Library/J.G. Fuller. 47 Hutchison Library/ Liba Taylor. 48-49 Hutchison Library/T.E. Clark. 49 Hutchison Library. 50 Hutchison Library/Nigel Howard. 51 Hutchison Library/ Nick Haslam. 52-53 Robert Harding/C. Bowman. 54-55 Hutchison Library/Liba Taylor. 55 Hutchison Library/ Vadim Kvorinin: T; Hutchison Library/Andrey Zvoznikov: B. 56-57 Hutchison Library/ Andrey Zvoznikov. 60 Hutchison Library/Robert Francis. 61 Hutchison Library/ Nigel Howard. 63 Hutchison Library/John Egan. 65 Hutchison Library/Nancy

Durrell McKenna. 66 Still Pictures/David Drain. 67 DRK/A. Kaye. 68 Anderson Geographics. 69 Robert Harding/I. Vanderharst. 70 Trip/Viesti Collection. 70-71 Hutchison Library. 72-73 Robert Harding. 74 Trip/Viesti Collection. 74-75 Trip/S. Grant. 75 Still Pictures/Peter Arnold Inc./Jeff Greenberg. 76 Still Pictures/Thomas Laird. 76-77 Robert Harding/Paul Van Riel. 77 Robert Harding. 78 Still Pictures/Julio Etchart. 78-79 DRK/Mark Gibson. 79 DRK/David Woodfall. 80 Trip/T. Freeman: T; Allsport/Clive Brunskill: B. 80-81 Allsport/Paul Severn. 82 Rex Features/Mike Segar. 82-83 Rex Features/Gary Calton. 84-85 DRK/Darrell Gulin: B. 85 Still Pictures/Jim Wark: T; NASA: B. 86 Popperfoto. 86-87 Rex Features/Alastair Pullen. 88 Robert Harding. 89 Rex Features/Sipa Press/Gustavo Ferrari. 90-91 Robert Harding: L; Hutchison Library/Nancy Durrell McKenna: R. 92 Robert Harding/J.C. Teyssier. 93 Hutchison Library/Brian Moser. 94 Trip/M. Shirley. 94-95 Robert Harding. 96 Still Pictures/John Cancalosi. 97 Hutchison Library/Juliet Highet: T; Hutchison Library/ Edward Parker: B. 98 Still Pictures/Mark Edwards. 98-99 Hutchison Library/ Robert Francis. 100-101 Hutchison Library/Philip Wolmuth. 101 Hutchison Library/Jeremy Horner. 102 Still Pictures/Paul Harrison. 102-103 Hutchison Library/John Hatt. 104-105 Hutchison Library/ Robert Francis. 106-107 Still Pictures/Nigel Harrison. 107 Still Pictures/ Jorgen Schytte. 108 Hutchison Library/Robert Francis. 112 Rex Features/Stewart Cook. 113 Still Pictures/Chris Martin. 114 Anderson Geographics. 115 Still Pictures/ Ron Giling. 116-117 Still Pictures/Josh Schachter. 117 Hutchison/Jeremy Horner. 118 Hutchison Library/Robert Francis. 118-119 Hutchison Library/Eric Lawrie. 119 Still Pictures/Ron Giling. 120-121 Hutchison Library/Robert

Francis. 121 Hutchison Library/ Jeremy Horner. 122 Still Pictures/John Maier. 122-123 Hutchison Library/ Jeremy Horner. 123 Hutchison Library/Richard House. 124 Still Pictures/John Maier. 124-125 Hutchison Library. 127 Still Pictures/Nigel Dickinson. 129 Still Pictures/ Muriel Nicolotti. 130 Anderson Geographics. 131-133 Hutchison Library/ Michael Macintyre. 133 Corbis/Paul Souders. 134-135 Still Pictures/John Isaacs: T; Robert Harding: B. 135 AFP/Corbis. 136 Corbis. 136-137 Corbis/Buddy Mays. 138 David Monfarrige. 138-139 Hutchison Library. 139 Popperfoto/Reuters. 140-141 Robert Harding. 141 Still Pictures/Demi-Unep. 142 Still Pictures/Ron Giling. 142-143 Hutchison Library. 143 Ron Giling/Still Pictures. 144 Robert Harding. 145 Still Pictures/Margaret Wilson. 146-147 Hutchison Library. 147 Popperfoto. 148 Steve McDonagh. 149 Hutchison Library: T; Corbis/David & Peter Turnley: B. 150 Still Pictures/Roger de la Harpe. 150-151 National Geographic Image Collection/Chris Johns. 161 Still Pictures/Ron Giling. 162-163 Anderson Geographics. 164-165 Corbis/ K.M. Westermann. 166 Hutchison Library/Nigel Howard. 166-167 Roy Williams. 167 Corbis/Reuters/New Media Inc. 168-169 Still Pictures/ Adrian Arbib. 169 Popperfoto/ Duncan Willetts: T; Still Pictures/Bojan Brecel: B. 170-171 Robert Harding/Tom Ang. 172-173 Robert Harding/ David Beatty. 173 Still Pictures/ Gil Moti. 174 Still Pictures/ Mark Edwards. 174-176 Michael Freeman. 177 Corbis/Popperfoto/Reuters. 178 Robert Harding. 179 Corbis/Jonathan Blair. 180-181 Still Pictures/John Isaacs. 182-183 Michael Freeman. 184 Still Pictures/ Ron Giling: T; Still Pictures/ Shehzad Nooran: B. 184-185 Popperfoto/Reuters/ Pawel Kopcynski. 186 Robert Harding/James Strachan. 186-187 Still

Pictures/Jean-Leo Dugas. 187 Still Pictures/Andy Crump. 193 Robert Harding/Explorer. 194-195 Still Pictures/Adrian Arbib. 196 Still Pictures/Ingrid Moorjohn. 196-197 Hutchison Library/Robert Francis. 198-199 Still Pictures/Julio Etchart. 199 Hutchison Library/Jeremy Horner. 200 Richard & Sally Greenhill. 201 Still Pictures. 202-203 Hutchison Library/ Maurice Harvey. 203 Hutchison Library/Robert Francis. 204 Robert Harding. 204-205 Hutchison Library/ Jon Burbank. 206 Hutchison Library/Jeremy Horner. 206-207 Hutchison Library/ Trevor Page. 208-209 Still Pictures/Jorgen Schytte. 209 Karen Aniola. 210 Still Pictures/Joerg Boethling. 211 Still Pictures/UNEP. 212-213 Karen Aniola. 213 Hutchison Library. 214-215 Still Pictures/Jorgen Scytte. 215 Still Pictures/Tim Page. 216-217 Hutchison Library/William Holtby. 218 Hutchison Library/ P. Collomb. 219 Karen Aniola. 220-221 Robert Harding/ N. Wheeler. 222 Still Pictures/ Tim Page. 223 Still Pictures/ Roland Seitre. 224-225 Anderson Geographics. 226-227 Hutchison Library/ Ian Lloyd. 227 Still Pictures/ Roland Seitre. 228-229 Still Pictures/John Cancalosi. 229 Hutchison Library. 230 Corbis/Robert Garvey. 230-231 Still Pictures/Roland Seitre. 232-233 Hutchison Library/Robert Francis. 234-235 Hutchison Library/ Nick Haslam. 235 Trip/ Ask Images. 236 Trip/Graham Pritchard. 236-237 Still Pictures/Vincent Bretagnolle. 237 Popperfoto. 238-239 Still Pictures/Yves Lefevre. 239 Still Pictures/Reportage/ Carlos Guarita. 240 Hutchison Library/Mary Jelliffe. 240-241 Still Pictures/Gerard & Margi Moss. 242-243 Still Pictures/Fred Bavendam. 243 Still Pictures/Andy Crump. 244 Still Pictures/Richard West. 244-245 Hutchison Library/ Bernard Regent. 246 Still Pictures/Dani/Jeske.

T = Top   L = Left
B = Bottom R = Right